NCMC
BS
1485.2
.S56
1996

D1189958

LOVING
AS
JESUS LOVES

A Devotional Exposition
of the Song of Songs

by

A.B. SIMPSON

CHRISTIAN PUBLICATIONS
CAMP HILL, PENNSYLVANIA

Christian Publications
3825 Hartzdale Drive, Camp Hill, PA 17011

Faithful, biblical publishing since 1883

ISBN: 0-87509-604-2
LOC Catalog Card Number: 95-70301
© 1996 by Christian Publications
All rights reserved
Printed in the United States of America

96 97 98 99 00   5   4   3   2   1

Unless otherwise indicated,
Scripture taken from the HOLY BIBLE,
NEW INTERNATIONAL VERSION®,
© 1973, 1978, 1984 by the International
Bible Society. Used by permission of
Zondervan Publishing House.
All rights reserved.

Loving as Jesus Loves
was formerly published under the title
The Love-Life of the Lord

CONTENTS

CHAPTER 1

Life of Love

From many standpoints the Bible looks at our spiritual life. Sometimes it is as a life of faith, sometimes as a life of holiness or as a life of service. Deepest of all the Bible looks at our life as a life of patience and victorious suffering. But the tenderest and most intimate forms, and the most exquisite figures of human affection and friendship are used to describe the unspeakable bond which links the heart of God with the souls He calls to be His own. It is not the love of compassion or the stronger love expressed by the relationship of fatherhood, brotherhood and even motherhood. It is the tie, above all others, which links two hearts in the exclusive affection which no other can share—the love of the bridegroom and the bride. This is the love which touches all human love with its inexpressible charm and transfigures and glorifies the humblest lot and the hardest circumstances into a heavenly paradise.

This is the meaning of the Song of Songs. This is the Old Testament climax of the series of figures that runs all the way from Eden to the Millennial throne.

The opening picture of the Bible is a love song—two hearts, the one born out of the other, and then given back to it in perfect unison, the central figures of earth's first Paradise. Next we have the story of Rebekah's wooing and Isaac's marriage, the great type of the heavenly Bridegroom sending to this far-off land for His chosen and exclusive bride. The beautiful idyll of Ruth and Boaz has the same figurative significance. The 45th Psalm is David's song of heavenly love and the divine Lover. Its tender call has reached many a Christian heart and called it to a heavenly betrothal, "Listen, O daughter, consider and give ear: Forget your people and your father's house. The king is enthralled by your beauty; honor him, for he is your lord" (Psalm 45:10-11).

The Bible's Love Song

This beautiful book is Solomon's love song. Later prophets re-echo its heavenly strains. Isaiah tells of our Maker who is our Husband. Jeremiah repeats the plaintive appeal, "I remember the devotion of your youth, how as a bride you loved me and followed me through the desert, through a land not sown" (2:2). Hosea tells of the higher experience, when the soul restored from its backslidings will call Him *Ishi*, "my husband," no longer Baali, "my master" (2:16). And He "will betroth [us to Him] in righteousness and justice, in love and compassion. [He] will betroth [us] in faithfulness, and [we] will acknowledge the LORD" (2:19-20).

Ezekiel vividly portrays the picture of the calling of the bride, "I passed by, and when I looked at you and saw that you were old enough for love, I spread the corner of my garment over you and covered your nakedness. I gave you my solemn oath and entered into a covenant with you, declares the Sovereign LORD, and you became mine" (16:8).

John the Baptist introduces Christ as the Bridegroom, while he himself is only the friend of the Bridegroom. Jesus takes up the figure Himself. Jesus speaks of His days as the time when the Bridegroom is with them, and of the days when He says that the Bridegroom will be taken away, and the waiting Bride will fast until His return. And, true to the figure, He commences His miracles at a marriage feast. His turning the water into wine was a type of the great purpose of His kingdom, to transform the earthly into the heavenly, and give to us not only the water of life but the wine of love.

His parables are as suggestive as His miracles. He tells of the marriage feast for the king's son, and the 10 virgins who went forth to meet the Bridegroom. Above all other New Testament writers, the apostle Paul catches the spirit of this exquisite figure and interprets the meaning of earthly affection by the heavenly reality. Speaking of the love of the husband and the wife, he lifts our thoughts above the earthly type to our deeper union with the Lord. With a depth and vividness of meaning that can scarcely be expressed in words and can only be understood by the heart that lies on the bosom of its Lord he says:

> This is a profound mystery—but I am talking about Christ and the church. (Ephesians 5:32)

> For the husband is the head of the wife as Christ is the head of the church, his body, of which he is the Savior. . . .
> Husbands, love your wives, just as Christ loved the church and gave himself up for her to make her holy, cleansing her by the washing with water through the word, and to present her to himself as a radiant church, without stain or wrinkle or any other blemish, but holy and blameless. In this same way, husbands ought to love their wives as their own bodies. He who loves his wife loves himself. After all, no one ever hated his own body, but he feeds and cares for it, just as Christ does the church—for we are members of his body. (5:23-30)

So again speaking of our personal purity, the very ground on which he urges it is our physical union with our Lord. "The body is . . . for the Lord, and the Lord for the body. . . . Do you not know that your bodies are members of Christ himself?" (1 Corinthians 6:13, 15).

The climax of all this heavenly imagery is reached in the book of Revelation where the universe is summoned to gaze on the crowning spectacle of God's love and power, the paragon of creation, redemption and grace, the wonder of angels, the delight of God.

"Come, I will show you the bride, the wife of the Lamb." (21:9)

Then I heard what sounded like a great multitude, like the roar of rushing waters and like loud peals of thunder, shouting:

"Hallelujah!
For our Lord God Almighty reigns.
Let us rejoice and be glad
and give him glory!
For the wedding of the Lamb has come,
and his bride has made herself ready.
Fine linen, bright and clean,
was given her to wear."
(Fine linen stands for the righteous acts of the saints.)

Then the angel said to me, "Write: 'Blessed are those who are invited to the wedding supper of the Lamb!' " And he added, "These are the true words of God." (19:6-9)

Surely, beloved, no man can say that a subject that occupies so prominent and sublime a place in God's holy Word and in the hopes of the future is unworthy of our profoundest interest and our most reverent and earnest consideration!

In oriental countries the marriage pageant is the chief event. The story that lies behind it is of less importance, for often the bridegroom and the bride never meet until for the first time he approaches her on her wedding day in all the splendor of her bridal robes, and, lifting the veil from her face, looks into her eyes. In our Christian civilization the marriage scene is the least important part of the entire proceedings. The love story of the heart and the tender and personal interest associated with the first acquaintance and ripening affection of wedded hearts after all the tests and triumphs of true love are over, this is the paramount importance. It is even so in the love story of the soul. Glorious, indeed, will be the hour when our love will be crowned and the bride of the Lamb will sit down by His side on His millennial throne. But far more important is the simple story of the call of the bride and the betrothal of the soul now to its everlasting Lord and Lover.

It is of this we mainly will speak in the consideration of our fascinating theme. And may it indeed prove, through the power of the Holy Spirit, in the case of many who will read these lines, the beginning of an everlasting love story that will invest all time and all eternity with an infinite and heavenly charm.

The Structure of Song of Songs

First, let us endeavor to grasp the structure of this book and the form of this beautiful drama in its simple beauty. It is a love song of the gifted and glorious king of Israel in the days of his purity, when his heart was true to God and true to his single bride. The heroine of canticles is known as Shulamith, or the daughter of Shulem which we know in Hebrew is the same as Shunem. I have never been able to resist the strong impression that she was the same maiden as we read of in connection with the closing days of David's life, the fairest daughter of Israel that could be found in all the land, who was especially brought to the aged king to be the companion of his closing days, to cheer and cherish by her sweetness and brightness the last moments of his feeble and sinking life.

We know that she was a daughter of Shunem. We know that she was so beautiful that she was selected for her surpassing loveliness. We know also that she was beloved of Adonijah, Solomon's faithless brother, and because he asked that she might be his bride, Solomon became strangely indignant and ordered his execution, saying that he might as well have asked the kingdom. One can hardly understand this indignation, unless, behind it, lay a secret in Solomon's heart of love to the fair Shulamite.

However this may be, it matters comparatively little. We are enabled, however, from the book itself, to weave a very complete thread of romantic and most suggestive incidents into one of the most charming of oriental poems. The plan of the story is very simple and will be best understood by dividing the book into six sections, which we may call respectively:

1. *The Waiting Days*

The first section, *the waiting days*, from chapter 1 to 2:7, represents the bride as waiting in the palace in Jerusalem with her maidens while preparing for her marriage. This is occupied with a number of little incidents comprising a song from her maidens, a chorus in which she joins, and then her interview and conversation with her lover as he suddenly appears and closes the song with mutual words of love, in one of the gardens of the palace.

2. *The Wooing Days*

Next, *the wooing days*, from chapter 2:8 to 3:5, contain the story of her wooing. It is told by her own lips in a little song to her maidens. She describes most beautifully the first visit of her lover to her rustic home under the shadows of Lebanon. And then it closes with a sad dream which followed his visit, in which it seemed to her as if she had lost his love, but at length she found him, welcomed him and brought him to her mother's home with a love which determined never again to let him go. Each of these beautiful scenes closes with the same simple refrain, "Daughters of Jerusalem, I charge you by the gazelles and by the does of the field: Do not arouse or awaken love until it so desires" (Song of Songs 3:5). This is a strong poetic expression denoting the intensity of her love and calling upon all to be careful how they thoughtlessly awaken the fires that burn with so intense a fervor.

3. The Wedding Days

Then come *the wedding days*, from chapter 3:6 to 5:1. This is the scene of the marriage procession, the words of love from the bridegroom to the bride and the wedding feast with the welcome to the guests.

4. The Testing Days

Next come *the testing days*, from chapter 5:2 to 8:10. This is the story of the trials which followed this happy union. They were the trials that began with her first failure, in her languor, self-indulgence and slowness to respond to the bridegroom's call. Then they were followed by sorrow and bitter repentance, and many an indignity from the watchmen of the street as she sought in vain for her lost bridegroom. But all through the separation her heart is true to him and her testimony unfaltering. She tells the daughters of Jerusalem of his beauty and loveliness, and still testifies without the shadow of a doubt, "I am my lover's and my lover is mine" (6:3). At length her faithfulness is rewarded, her trials are ended and her lover returns and meets her with words of unbounded affection, admiration and comfort. Her maidens look upon her with wondering delight as she appears before them with new beauty. "Fair as the moon, bright as the sun, majestic as the stars in procession" (6:10). The scene closes with a still closer union and a more complete expression of her utter surrender to his will in the simple words, deeper than any she had yet expressed, "I belong to my lover, and his desire is for me" (7:10). It is not now, "My lover is mine." The selfishness even of her love is gone, and her one thought is to be his and to meet his every wish for her.

5. *Home Longings*

The thought of this section is best expressed by the words *home longings*. It is the cry of her heart for her old home (8:2-4). This is not a selfish desire, nor merely a lonesome, homesick wish to be back in her mother's house once more, nor to be absent from her lover. Rather it is a wish to have him more wholly to herself out of the excitement and confusion of the city, and the causes that so often separate him from her, in the simple unbroken communion of her own home. It is a longing for the days when he used to be ever by her side among the Galilean hills. It is the cry of a loving heart for constant, unbroken fellowship and separation from others unto him alone.

6. *Homecoming*

Chapter 8:5-14 presents the *homecoming*. It is the beautiful picture of the fulfillment of her longing: the return to Galilee, the renewal of their plighted vows under the old trees and amid the old trysting scenes. Then comes her artless yet half-artful intercession for her sisters and her brother, and that all dear to her may share in the blessing which she enjoys. The beautiful scene closes with the request of her bridegroom for a favor from her, and that is that she will sing for him one of the songs which doubtless she had often sung in the days of old. The poem closes with her last song, a sweet out-breathing of the love that longs for his presence, and that asks only for him in inseparable union, pointing forward in its deep spiritual application to the everlasting song and the undivided fellowship of the home above.

The Application

Such is the structure of this love story, and it is easy to see how much may lie back of it in the higher world of spiritual realities. Of course there is boundless room for extravagant and visionary application, but there is also abundant cause for sober, scriptural interpretation and for lessons that touch the whole field of personal experience and dispensational truth.

Jewish writers have been very fond of seeing in it the story of their race, and much that they have seen is doubtless true, perhaps all. Most truthfully and vividly does it recall the beginning of their history—waiting like her in the king's palace in the time of Solomon's magnificence and splendor, unequaled and apparently unlikely to be ever changed. The story of her wooing is the story of God's loving call to ancient Israel, as He summoned them to come with Him to another land

and accept Him as their heavenly Husband. The first sad dream of chapter 2 is applied to the dark days of the Babylonian captivity. The second and more terrible dream, and the longer separation of chapter 5, with all the wrongs received at the watchmen's hands, has been more than fulfilled in the sad story of the Middle Ages and the sufferings of the Jewish nation for nearly 1800 years. The reason for this is not hard to find in the confession of the bride. It was because God had knocked at Israel's door and been rejected when He came to them as their Bridegroom in the days of His flesh. But He will appear to them once more, as Solomon did to his beloved, and, as in her case, so for them also there will be the restoration to the old home once more, and amid the hills of Galilee and the scenes of Hebrew history will He renew with them His everlasting covenant and betroth them unto Himself forever, and Israel's last song will be "the song of Moses . . . and the song of the Lamb" (Revelation 15:3).

The application of this delightful allegory to the church of Christ is still more marked. She, too, had her waiting and her call to come out from the world and follow her Lord according to the beautiful imagery of chapter 2:8-13. And with His call came a new springtime and an everlasting summer. She, too, had her first dark dream, perhaps during the sad days of His crucifixion and burial. She, too, had her spiritual betrothal and marriage to her Lord and went forth in pentecostal power and apostolic purity in His name, and with all the fullness of His gifts and graces, and the fellowship of His love. But she, too, like Israel, has had her second and her longer sad dream of sorrow and separation, in the dark ages of error and corruption, which almost blotted out the church for a thousand years from existence. And she, too, has had her restoration and once more has begun to appear in the glory of His spiritual revealing, "fair as the moon, bright as the sun, majestic as the stars in procession" (Song of Songs 6:10). And above all, like the fair bride when restored to His spiritual fellowship, her great longing and blessed hope is His personal coming and the restitution of all things which that coming is to bring. This corresponds to the bride's return to her Galilean home. And her sweetest song and the song the Bridegroom loves the best is that which every true heart is singing today, and which is the closing echo of the Bible itself, "Make haste, my beloved" (8:14, KJV), or, as the New Testament translates it, "Come, Lord Jesus, come quickly."

A Personal Application

But Solomon's song has a very special application to the individual Christian.

We see in it the story of our call, conversion and justification. "Take me away with you—let us hurry! Let the king bring me into his chambers" (1:4). This is where we all began. "Dark am I, yet lovely, O daughters of Jerusalem, dark like the tents of Kedar, like the tent curtains of Solomon" (1:5). This is the striking picture of the soul's justification. Sinful and unworthy, in ourselves, we yet are clothed in our Savior's spotless righteousness, and "beautiful through His comeliness." Our righteousness is not our own; but clothed in His merits and united to His person we are "even as He."

We see the soul's desire for a deeper intimacy with Jesus. "Tell me, you whom I love, where you graze your flock and where you rest your sheep at midday. Why should I be like a veiled woman beside the flocks of your friends?" (1:7). It is the cry of the hungry heart for the living bread and of the tired spirit for the secret place of His presence and His rest. And He answers it by the revelation of His love, so that the happy heart can say, "I delight to sit in his shade, and his fruit is sweet to my taste. He has taken me to the banquet hall, and his banner over me is love" (2:3-4).

This is more than the call to leave all and follow Him. The relation of Jesus to the disciples on the banks of Jordan brought them to His house to abide with Him that whole day. But there came another call, a little later, to leave all and follow Him forever. This is the call of the second scene in the Song of Songs. "Arise, come, my darling; my beautiful one, come with me" (2:13). Happy are they who promptly answer, "I will go."

We see the soul a little reluctant to respond to so abrupt a call, and putting him off a little while "until the day breaks" (2:17). But also it is followed by a bitter disappointment, and a sad and gloomy night, when she seeks her lord long in vain, and at last is only too glad to find him even on the streets, and bring him to her home to be parted no more.

Next we see the soul's marriage to the Lord, in the imagery of the third and fourth chapters.

This is the great spiritual mystery of grace, the union of the heart with Christ in the happy hour, when all has been yielded and the Holy Spirit comes to say, "You will be called Hephzibah, and your land Beulah; for the LORD will take delight in you, and your land will be married" (Isaiah 62:4).

Then come the testing days of the heart when faith and love are tried and even failures come to teach us deeper lessons and establish us in a place of strength that we never knew before. First he leaves his bride for a little, but it is only till the evening, and soon he returns with tenderest love. Next he comes at night to her door, but she is asleep and waits so long to open the door that he goes away again. Then comes the darkest of her trials. She seeks him but she finds him not. The watchmen of the street insult and mock her. But she is steadfastly faithful to her lord. She declares to all his glory and his grace. She declares her own love to him. At last he appears to her, and with words of tenderest affection rewards her constancy and love. And then she appears in a loveliness and glory she had never known before. Her trials have only deepened her life, and now she "appears like the dawn, fair as the moon, bright as the sun, majestic as the stars in procession" (Song of Songs 6:10). And so wholly his has she become that her one testimony is, "I belong to my lover, and his desire is for me" (7:10).

Such is the soul's experience often even after it has come into full union with its Lord. A very slight unfaithfulness will often bring a long, sad separation and many a sorrow. It is a much more serious thing to disobey Christ after we have come into full union with Him than before. But even this sad failure is not irremediable. Out of these testings we come with an experience worth all it cost, and a consecration that can say without reserve, "I am my Beloved's and want to meet His desire and satisfy His love to me."

The later experiences of Shulamith have their counterpart in every true spiritual life. The longing to dwell apart with Him, the cry for His closer presence, the longing for home, especially for His blessed coming again—all these things are the ripening of the love life of the heart and the preparation for His coming. The more we know Him spiritually, the more will we long to see Him face to face, and to be with Him where distance doesn't divide, and temptation, sin and sorrow come no more.

CHAPTER 2

Waiting Days

He has taken me to the banquet hall, and his banner over me is love. (Song of Songs 2:4)

As we have already seen, the Song of Songs opens with the picture of the bride waiting in the palace of the king for her wedding day. She has come from her Galilean home and is surrounded by her attendants, the daughters of Jerusalem. The poem opens with a song by her, and a chorus in which her maidens join, occupying the first eight verses. This is followed by another solo, in which she calls upon her lover to tell her where she may find him. Then there is a response by her maidens, who bid her go forth and search by the footsteps of the flocks. Then her lover himself appears, and the rest of the scene is a conversation between them in one of the arbors of the king's gardens, followed by a repast in the banquet hall of the palace. The whole scene is full of spiritual parallels, reminding us of our own most precious experience.

Her Heavenly Call

We have her heavenly call. "Take me away with you—let us hurry! Let the king bring me into his chambers" (Song of Songs 1:4). She recognizes even her love as the response of her heart to another love that first drew her. How true of us! "We love because he first loved us" (1 John 4:19).

"By the grace of God I am what I am" (1 Corinthians 15:10). With loving-kindness Jesus Christ has drawn us because He loves us with an everlasting love. Our highest longings after God were first inspired in us by God Himself, and we never "take hold of" more than "that for which Christ Jesus took hold of" us (Philippians 3:12). Well may we say of that great love that had anticipated long ago all that it has brought us, and much more that is to follow:

How precious to me are your thoughts, O
     God!
How vast is the sum of them!
Were I to count them,
     they would outnumber the grains of
sand.
          (Psalm 139:17-18)

Because of His great love for us, God, who is rich in mercy, made us alive with Christ even when we were dead in transgressions—it is by grace you have been saved. And God raised us up with

Christ and seated us with him in the
heavenly realms in Christ Jesus.
(Ephesians 2:4-6)

Her Heavenly Robes

"Dark am I, yet lovely, . . . like the tents of
Kedar, like the tent curtains of Solomon" (Song
of Songs 1:5). That is: "I am black as the tents of
Kedar, as beautiful as the curtains of Solomon."

We have here a beautiful blending of perfect
humility and perfect confidence. This is the
spirit which should run through our entire
Christian life. True first of the sinner's justification, it will ever be as true of the saint's holiness.
It is practically Paul's own confession, "the chief
of sinners, but I obtained mercy" (see 1 Timothy 1:13, 15). "Not that we are competent in
ourselves to claim anything for ourselves, but
our competence comes from God" (2 Corinthians 3:5).

It is the lowliness that prostrates itself in the
dust, evermore conscious even after the longest
experience of Christ's grace, that we still are
nothing but worthless empty vessels, and that all
our righteousness is not self-constituted but con-
stantly dependent on Christ alone. It is just because our righteousness is not our own that we
can speak of it in such high terms, and dare to
say, "I am lovely; I am clothed with the righteousness of Jesus: I am kept by the power of
God; 'I can do all things through Christ which
strengtheneth me' " (Philippians 4:13, KJV).

"He has clothed me with the robes of his righteousness. I am sanctified by Christ Jesus and filled with the Holy Spirit, and enabled to walk with Him in holy obedience unto all pleasing, and yet I am nothing by myself. But, 'by the grace of God I am what I am' " (1 Corinthians 15:10). And His "grace . . . was poured out on me abundantly, along with the faith and love that are in Christ Jesus" (1 Timothy 1:14).

There is no modesty in sitting down in the kitchen if we are the sons of God and the beloved of our Father's family. He expects us, with becoming dignity, to take the place His love has given us and to feel at home in the heavenly robes in which His grace has arrayed us. He dares us to say, as He says of us, "The blood of Jesus, his Son, purifies us from all sin" (1 John 1:7).

Her Higher Longings

She had higher longings—for her Lord Himself. It was not enough for her to be in His palace and arrayed in His robes of loveliness and honor, but she wanted her Lover Himself. "Tell me," she cries, "you whom I love, where you graze your flock and where you rest your sheep at midday. Why should I be like a veiled woman beside the flocks of your friends?" (Song of Songs 1:7). She cannot be content with the society of others, nor can any of them be her shepherd. Three things she wants in Him. She wants Him to feed her; she wants Him to rest her; and she wants Him to be her companion and give her His sweet society.

1. Her Cry for Food

This expresses the soul's deep longing for a closer fellowship with Jesus. Its first cry is for His love to minister to its deep need, "Tell me where you graze." The spirit has its own peculiar capacities and needs, and Christ alone can satisfy them. He is our living bread. "The one who feeds on me will live because of me" (John 6:57). "For my flesh is real food and my blood is real drink. Whoever eats my flesh and drinks my blood remains in me, and I in him" (6:55-56). "Unless you eat the flesh of the Son of Man and drink his blood, you have no life in you" (6:53).

This is the source of spiritual freshness, gladness and growth. This is the spring of physical healing and victorious life in every sense. Without this, Christian work will soon exhaust us. We are as dependent upon Him as the babe upon its mother's breast. The restlessness, frets and failures of most Christians arise from the lack of spiritual nourishment and not knowing "where He feeds His flock." But nobody can tell you the secret but Him.

The daughters of Jerusalem could not answer the question any more than John the Baptist could tell Andrew and Simon where the Master dwelt. He Himself had to take them home to His own abode and welcome them to His inner fellowship. If you want to know the secret of abiding in Jesus and feeding upon His life, go to Him and tell Him, like Shulamith, your desire. And although you may not see Him at the time nor feel His presence, although He may be absent from your consciousness as Solomon was from hers, still you can stretch out your hands in the darkness and breathe out your cry in His ear as she did, "Tell me . . . where do you rest your sheep at midday" (Song of Songs 1:7). And He will be by your side, as He was by hers, answering the longing of her heart. The only way to Jesus is Jesus Himself. The answerer of your hard questions, the light of the blind as well as the life from the dead is He who is the Alpha and the Omega, the First and the Last.

2. Her Cry for Rest

The next cry is for rest. This is the deep need of the heart in this world of change and in the midst of constant irritation, opposition, toil and sorrow. The human spirit finds no rest in earthly things and has an instinctive longing for the deep repose which only God can give. This is the sweet blessing Christ has purchased for us. It was the legacy which He especially mentioned when leaving His beloved ones, "Peace I leave with you; my peace I give you" (John 14:27). And this peace must ever come to us on His bosom. Our only resting place is His heart. It is He who rests His flock at noon. It is beautiful that the rest comes at the hottest, hardest hour of the day. It is when the sun is beating most fiercely from the tropical sky. It is when all life is languishing under its fiery breath that He holds His own upon His breast at noon as under the "shadow of a great rock in a thirsty land" (Isaiah 32:2). Oh, the peace Jesus gives! It passes all understanding. They who come to Him indeed find rest unto their souls.

Friend, do you not long for God's quiet, the inner chambers, the shadow of the Almighty, the secret of His presence? Your life perhaps has been all driving and doing, or perhaps straining, struggling, longing and not obtaining. Oh, for rest! To lie down upon His bosom and know that you have all in Him, that every question is answered, every doubt settled, every interest safe, every prayer answered, every desire satisfied. It is God's everlasting rest. You may have it. Lift up the cry, "Tell me, you whom I love, where do you graze your flock and where you rest your sheep at midday" (Song of Songs 1:7).

3. Her Cry for Companionship and Love

The last longing of the heart is for his companionship and his love. The very cry is addressed to him whom her soul loved. Her appeal is for the love that will make her his exclusive object and separate her from his companions. It is not their society she wants but his. Oh, how we need to be separated from people, even the best, and have such direct contact with Him that they will be dear to us only through Him. In His blessed society we will not even need any other, should He so order it, but Himself. And if He does link us, as

He so sweetly does, with His own, they will be reckoned as part of Him and will minister to us not in their human love, but the love and life of Jesus.

Blessed be His name! He has this for us, His exclusive love, a love which each individual somehow feels is all for himself, in which he can lie alone upon His breast and have a place which none other can dispute. And yet His heart is so great that He can hold a thousand million just as near. Yet each heart can possess Him as exclusively for its own even as the thousand little pools of water upon the beach can reflect the sun, and each little pool seem to have a whole sun embosomed in its beautiful depths.

Only Christ can teach us this secret of His inmost love. It is an old story that nobody else can cause love for you but yourself. Marriages are made in China by middlemen but true hearts are not thus wedded, nor can you learn it out of a book. It has to be the spontaneous prompting of a loving heart. So Christ alone can unlock the secret door of love and wholly possess the heart as His shrine.

Her Happy Experience

Finally we see her happy experience and the satisfaction of all her heart's desire.

Her cry is not in vain. The echoes have scarcely died away when her beloved is by her side with words of affection and admiration and the unbroken fellowship of his love. Her own glad testimony tells the story of the completeness of the answer which he brings to all her heart's desire. Had she longed for rest? "I delight," she says, "to sit in his shade" (Song of Songs 2:3). For his heavenly feeding, "his fruit is sweet to my taste. He has taken me to the banquet hall" (2:3-4). For his more precious love, "his banner over me is love" (2:4).

So He wants to give us rest, to cover us with His shadow, to make us to sit down under it with great delight. But we must sit down if we would know His rest. We must cease from our own activity and we must be willing to go into the shadow, lost to the sight of ourselves, lost to the sight of others, overshadowed by what they might call gloom or even shadow. But it is the shadow of the Almighty, and oh, the delight of those who there sit down and trust where they cannot see! The most that we need to do to get rest is simply to rest. We need to cease from what we are thinking, questioning, planning, fearing. We need to suppress ourselves, to stop thinking, to stop trying, to stop listening, to stop answering the tempter. We need to hide our heads on the bosom of Jesus and let Him think and love and keep, seeing nothing but the shadow of our Beloved, which hides everything else, even the light of our way, from our view.

And He has for us the heavenly fruit and the house of wine. "His fruit is sweet to my taste." Not the fruit He gives but the fruit He bears; He is the apple tree and we feed on Him. The banquet hall literally means the house of wine, and wine is the scriptural symbol of life, of blood, of the richest form of life. He feeds us upon His very life. He gives us, not only the sacramental cup but every other, and says of it, "Drink from it, all of you" (Matthew 26:27).

And finally, He is for us the satisfaction of our love. "His banner over me is love" (Song of Songs 2:4). This means, of course, that His love for us is the pledge and guarantee of our safety and protection. What can harm us if God be for us? His love defies every foe and secures every resource. But the words have a deeper meaning.

They suggest that our banner, too, is love. The power that will guard us, the defense that will save us from all evils and keep us in perfect victory is that which is the spirit and theme of all this song, the love life of the Lord. Its design is to teach us that love life that is above every other life. It is when we are baptized into its perfect love, when our beings are penetrated and filled with this heavenly principle that we are bannered against all our foes and armed for perfect victory. Love is the weapon, even more than faith, that will disarm all our enemies and melt their fiery darts into harmless weakness as they strike our glowing breastplate of love.

Archimedes who proposed to destroy the ships of the enemy by a simple burning glass, through which he converged upon them the rays of the sun and set them on fire. The love of the Lord, burning in our hearts, will consume everything that harms us. Satan cannot live against it a moment. It consumes all our enemies and turns their hatred into love. It is the antidote to every temptation that can come to us in disobedience and unfaithfulness. It is the charm that inspires and sustains every sacrifice and service for the Lord and makes every burden light. It is the balm that brings even healing to our flesh and mortal frame. It is the joy of the earth and light of heaven.

CHAPTER 3

Wooing Days

Arise, come, my darling; my beautiful one, come with me. (Song of Songs 2:13)

This is the story of the calling of the bride. It is recited as a sort of song or soliloquy. Perhaps it was told to the attendant maiden as she waited in the palace for her wedding day. Her home had been amid the beautiful scenes of northern Galilee, somewhere among the foothills of Lebanon. There in her simple rustic home, with her mother and her brothers (her father is not mentioned and she was probably an orphan girl), she had lived in seclusion. She even labored with her hands in taking care of her brothers' vineyards. Her beauty, however, had attracted the notice of Solomon. He had found her out in her quiet home and the story of his coming is here described with great vividness and beauty.

The Story

Appearing at her lattice-window one day in the springtime, doubtless after his first acquaintance had given him the right to make such a visit, he whispered the startling call to her to leave her lowly home and come away with him into a sweeter springtime of love.

> See! The winter is past;
>   the rains are over and gone.
> Flowers appear on the earth;
>   the season of singing has come,
> the cooing of doves
>   is heard in our land.
> The fig tree forms its early fruit;
>   the blossoming vines spread their
>   fragrance.
> Arise, come, my darling;
>   my beautiful one, come with me.
>   (Song of Songs 2:11-13)

And as she coyly hid away he pleaded, "My dove in the clefts of the rock, in the hiding places on the mountainside, show me your face" (2:14).

The words that follow seem to be a request to her to sing for him one of her simple country songs, which she does in the playful strains of the 15th verse. "Catch for us the foxes, the little foxes that ruin the vineyards, our vineyards that are in bloom" (2:15).

Perhaps she meant in her little song to put him off in half playful mood or invite him to come and help her in the care of the garden, as her duties were more practical than he seemed to imagine. Instead of going with him it would be more fitting for him to come and help her in the care of her vineyard and catch for her the little foxes that eluded her ability. But at the same time she sings softly to herself in an undertone, perhaps not meant altogether for him, "My lover is mine and I am his" (2:16). Then she resumes her little song again in the 17th verse, gently hinting to him to withdraw for a little until the morning and the shadows flee away, and then to swiftly come from the mountains of division which are to separate them for a little while. In a word it is a quiet hint to him to come back at another time when perhaps they will be less exposed to curious eyes and she less busy with her practical duties.

Then follows the sad dream of the third chapter. That night was a very lonely and gloomy one and in her sleep she thought she had lost her beloved whom she had thus foolishly sent away. "All night long on my bed I looked for the one my heart loves; I looked for him but did not find him" (3:1).

Next she tells how she went forth into the city and sought him in the streets in vain. She explains how she went to the watchmen for direction. At last after a painful search, she found him and she gladly welcomed him and brought him to her mother's home. She didn't fear to have the world know her love because she would thus atone for the folly which before had let him go. This is the beautiful story of the call of this ancient bride, and back of it lie the deeper teach-

ings of our spiritual life and the experiences of
many of us.

The Coming of the Beloved

This is a picture of the Savior's coming to the
heart which He calls to the fullness of His love. It
looks back to His first coming to save a ruined
world. He is represented as coming upon the
mountains and leaping over the hills. What mountains of sin, hills of provocation, obstacles that
nothing but infinite power and love could ever
have surmounted. Oh the hindrances which our
depravity, which our prejudices, which our will-
fulness have placed between His love and our
wicked hearts, but how swiftly and victoriously
He came!

> Down from the shining hosts above
>   With joyful haste He sped.

To each of us has He come. He has sought us
with His whole heart. How touching the picture
of His standing behind the wall looking at the
windows, showing Himself at the lattice. It tells of
Him who has waited long to gain our attention, to
win our confidence, to reach our hearts. He is still
crying to many of us, "Here I am! I stand at the
door and knock. If anyone hears my voice and
opens the door, I will come in and eat with him,
and he with me" (Revelation 3:20).

His Call

"My lover spoke and said to me, 'Arise, my darling, my beautiful one, and come with me' " (Song of Songs 2:10).

This is the Master's call to do something and to leave something. We will never get anywhere in the life of consecration until we take a positive step and positive stand. We must rise up sometimes. The act of rising up in the congregation and committing one's self to a consecrated life is often the first real step in a life of holiness. But whatever the step, there is something that must be done before we can make any headway, and there is something that must be left. We must "come away" (KJV). There are associations from which we must break away, worldly entanglements that we must separate from, forbidden occupations that we must abandon, doubtful relationships that we must dissolve, pleasures that we must forsake, friends that we must surrender. "Therefore come out from them and be separate, says the Lord. Touch no unclean thing and I will receive you" (2 Corinthians 6:17) is the peremptory condition of the promise. "I will be a Father to you, and you will be my sons and daughters, says the Lord Almighty" (6:18).

And, therefore, we must go somewhere. At least we must go with Him wherever He may go.

I will follow Jesus,
Anywhere, everywhere, I will follow on.

It is enough to know that He leads; enough to be with Him. Friend, have you answered this call, "Rise up and come away?" This is speaking to some of us today, as it finds us in some forbidden place. It bids us to decide like Rebekah when the servant of Abraham brought her the proposal to be the wife of Isaac and they pressed the solemn question for her immediate decision, "Will you go with this man?" And she answered, "I will go" (Genesis 24:58). He was a stranger to her. The land to which he led her was a strange land. She did not know the way. She had not even seen her bridegroom, but her trusting heart accepted it all without reserve, and her prompt decision was, "I will go." When the soul thus answers to the call of Jesus it has begun an everlasting progression of blessing and glory.

So He is calling you today, "Rise up and come away." Come from this perishing world. Come from the low claims of your selfish life. Come out from the fellowship of the worldly. Come out from the hopes that end with earth. Put your hand in His. Commit your future to His will. Invest all your hopes in His kingdom and coming. And you will find how true it is, "Whoever loses his life for my sake will find it" (Matthew 10:39).

His Pleading

He urges her to come by all the beauty and gladness of the world around. He no doubt means this as a type of the brighter springtime and summer of happiness and love into which He is to introduce her. Much more true is this of our heavenly Bridegroom's call. The summer land of love into which He brings us is one whose beauty no springtide glory can express and no sunlit sky adequately set forth.

Oh, that we may hear His pleading and that we too may have cause to sing,

> I've reached the land of Beulah,
>   the summer land of love,
> Land of the Heavenly Bridegroom,
>   land of the Holy dove.
> My winter has departed,
>   my summer time has come.
> The air is full of singing,
>   the earth is bright with bloom.
> Oh! blessed land of Beulah,
>   sweet summer land of love.
> Oh! blessed Heavenly Bridegroom,
>   Oh! gentle Holy dove.
> Oh! Saviour keep us ever,
>   all earth-born things above,
> In the blessed land of Beulah,
>   the summer land of love.

The winter is past. It stands for the coldness, the barrenness and the wretchedness of our old selfish life. It is the first-bound misery and the selfishness in which we do dwell until the warm Sun of Righteousness lights up our life with heavenly radiance and melts our frigid hearts to love and sweetness. The coming of Christ to the heart is like a great thaw. Not so great is the difference between December and May, as between the earthbound heart and the soul into which Christ has come to reign.

The rain is over and gone. This is the figure of clouds, mists, spiritual darkness and gloom. Many Christians live in an atmosphere where they never see the sun. It is all mists and tears, doubts and fears, clouds and cares. But when we follow Him the rain is over and gone, the sky is ever clear, the sun is ever bright, the face of our Lord is ever unclouded and unveiled. Our sun will no more go down nor our moon withdraw her shining, for the Lord will be our everlasting light and the days of our mourning will be ended.

The flowers appear on the earth. Blossoms are the beautiful earthly types of faith; the flower is just the promise of the fruit. It is nature anticipating the coming seed and running over with the joy of the anticipation. The flower is just a fruit in embryo, and so faith is just the bud and blossom which foretells the coming blessing. How full of luxuriant beauty and blossom God has made the summertime of the world. Blossoms are everywhere. Wild flowers are running to waste on every mountainside and wayside and in the wilderness where no eye ever sees them but the insects and the birds. God's prodigal hand scatters them everywhere, for the delight of His own heart and the joy of the meanest creatures that gaze upon their beauty.

So God wants our lives to effloresce in the overflowing beauty and luxuriance which will not only fill up the actual routine of duty, but which will run over in such fullness that we will be a blessing to every creature we touch. Even the insects that buzz around us, the sparrows that play on the sidewalk or at the door, the birds that sing in our branches, our own dog will be the better and the happier for our religion and will almost know that something has happened to us. An engineer re-marked the other day that since he had become a consecrated Christian his old engine seemed to know it and went better. When it didn't work cor-rectly he used to swear at it, but now he only lifted his heart and voice in a word of prayer or a note of song, and the old engine tried to keep time, as the piston moved apace with his song and seemed to say "Amen!"

When we follow Christ in all His fullness, then our heart will be a land of flowers; our life a gar-den of bloom.

The time of the singing of the birds is come. Rather, the time of singing is come. The spirit of praise is one of the signs of a consecrated life. We pray less and sing more. Certainly we groan less, or rather we turn all our murmurs and moans into hallelujahs and life is one sweet ever-lasting song. Sorrow cannot quench it, but we count it all joy even when we cannot see or feel the joy.

Friend, God is calling you to a life of song. You do not praise enough, and you never will until you know the love life of the Lord. Then the song will be like a nightingale in the house. It will sing at midnight because it cannot help it. It will sing when there seems no rational cause for singing. It will sing just because the song is there and it must sing even amid the darkness, the raging tempest or with the dirges of death and despair on every side.

The voice of the dove is heard in our land—that is the sweet emblem of the Holy Spirit. How beautiful the notes of the wood dove as some of us remember them in our childhood, sometimes on some distant mountainside. How much more beautiful as they ring, "through all Judea's echoing land." This is the sweet symbol of the gentle and peaceful voice of the Holy Spirit as it is revealed to the listening ear of love. Oh, how delightful the first whisper of a Comforter in our hearts, sorrowing perhaps, or lonely and afraid. Oh, can we ever forget the blissful moment when the voice of the dove was first heard in our land. All heaven seemed to whisper, "Peace! Peace!" and the heart nestled under the wings of the heavenly Dove. The soul grew still as it hearkened to the still, small voice that said, "Peace I leave with you; my peace I give you. I do not give to you as the world gives. Do not let your hearts be troubled and do not be afraid" (John 14:27). Friend, follow Jesus and you will know the voice of the dove, the peace that passes all understanding, the heavenly presence that folds you under the wings of everlasting love and stills you in the eternal calm of the bosom of God.

Let us not fail to notice the words *"in our land"* (Song of Songs 2:12). The voice of the dove is not heard in the old land of self-love and sin, but only in the land to which our Bridegroom calls us—the land of love and fellowship with God. How sweetly He calls it "our land." He does not say

"My land." Already He recognizes the partnership to which He has called us and shares with us even the better country into which we have not yet entered. Friend, let us make it our land too.

Living in the Springtime

There is one way of living in everlasting spring, even on this little globe. That is, like the birds of passage, to fly away when the winter comes and leave the land of winter for southern climes where frosts are not and cold blasts never blow. How sweetly William Cowper sings to one of these happy birds that live in continual sunshine.

> Sweet bird, thy heart is ever young,
> Thy voice is ever clear;
> Thou hast no sorrow in thy song,
> No winter in thy year.

This may be true of the heart that will migrate from the winterland of the old life to the everlasting summer of His presence. There is such a land of love and peace for every weary, homesick heart. Friend, let us arise and come away. The voice of the dove is calling us to do it.

"The fig tree forms its early fruit" (2:13). The fruit has been hanging all the winter on the tree, and they are green and sour, but with the springtime they ripen and become aromatic and mellow. As the beautiful Hebrew phrase expresses it, "She spiceth forth her green figs."

How true of the Christian life. The ordinary Christian has figs, but they are winter figs. They are green and sour. He does something for God and has many a good feeling, but there is no perfume about it. It is raw and harsh. But when love comes, and the love life of the Lord possesses all the being, oh, how mellow the spirit becomes. How tender the unction. How gentle the meekness and patience. How fervid the zeal and the love. How full of fragrance, how spiced with heavenly sweetness the whole being and bearing become!

"The blossoming vines spread their fragrance" (2:13). This is higher than fruit. It is fragrance, the very smell of the plant. It is that which, as we will see later in this beautiful song, is the highest expression of spiritual qualities, and the flavor of the Christian spirit. Many Christians have fruit, but they have no fragrance. There is much value in their lives, but there is no attractiveness. This is not as God would have it. He wants the vines with the tender grapes to spread a nice aroma, and this never can be until our whole being is saturated with love. This love, then, must first come from the love of the Lord, revealed to us, accepted by us and reflected from our happy, heavenly lives.

His Repeated Call

Once again He calls His beloved one. "My dove in the clefts of the rock, in the hiding places on the mountainside, show me your face, let me hear your voice" (2:14). She had been turning away, and he pleads with her to turn back and let him look upon her face and hear her voice.

Christ wants us to turn our faces directly to Him. Is not this the attitude of prayer, and the prayer that looks up into the face of God with unveiled countenance and loving, whole-hearted confidence? God wants our faces turned heavenward, and shining with the reflected glory of the skies. Too often we go with faces turned downward and earthward, but He says, "Let me see your face."

Lift up your face toward the heavens, for He wants to hear your voice in holy testimony and praise. Not until you give Him your voice and fully confess Him with your lips will you know all the fullness of His deeper abiding. He wants your lips to answer His question and to testify to His love. The reason that many Christians have never had the full witness of His Spirit is because their face has never fully witnessed unto Him. Friend, let Him hear your voice.

Her Response

Her answer was not worthy of His love. There was a little trifling in it, a little procrastination, and yet a good deal of sincere love, but enough hesitation and compromise to lose her full blessing. Her playful hint to him to come and catch the foxes that spoiled the vines was a little like the excuse that some of us make when Christ calls us to be all His own, that we are too busy with our earthly duties for what we sometimes consider sentimental religion. And that when we get a little more leisure from our secular cares and occupations we will give our attention to a life of devotion. That is the very time and place that we need our Lord the most.

He is indeed willing to come into our common life and help us with our vines and little foxes—but not until we have first surrendered them to Him so fully that we are at leisure from them for His other calls, not until we are willing to turn aside from the most engrossing occupation to commune with Him or to follow Him wherever He may lead.

Her great mistake, however, was the procrastination and delay which put Him off until the evening. Perhaps it was the shame of being seen with Him which prompted her proposal. Perhaps it was the pressing cares of the day. But whatever it was, it was wholly wrong and cost her a very sorrowful night. How often many of us are tempted to say, "Go away for a time."

The children of Israel, when called by God to enter the promised land, hesitated only for a night. They were quite willing the next morning to follow the pillar of cloud from Kadesh Barneah had it led that way, but it was too late. God refused to go with them. Now it was their time, but it was not His. The time of His visitation was passed. Love brooks no delay. Oh, that each of us might be able to say of every call of the heavenly voice, When He said "Seek My face," my heart replied, "Your face, LORD, I will seek" (Psalm 27:8).

A hint is enough to repel a sensitive heart. Love is peculiarly sensitive, and the Holy Spirit is easily offended and grieved from our door. Let us take heed how we chill His overtures and appeals by even a qualified refusal. Let our whole heart ever meet Him as generously and uncompromisingly as He has given all to us.

The Sad Sequel

Her reluctant response brings a sad sequel. The sorrowful dream which follows in the sad story of Shulamith, is also the story of many a Christian heart. "All night long . . . I looked for him but did not find him" (Song of Songs 3:1). The grieved friend withdraws, and the heart is conscious of desertion and loneliness and awakes to realize its terrible mistake. But still there is something we can do. We can seek Him as she did, and when we find Him not, we can, as she did, go to the watchmen and ask the way. They can tell us the way, but they cannot take us to Him. We must go beyond them. It was not until she passed the watchmen that she found her beloved. And it is not until we pass beyond the presence and the consciousness of even the best of men, and even those who have helped us most to find our Lord, that we really find Him. The lover always meets his loved one alone. No friend can be witness of the trysting hour. Heart to heart, and with no other heart between, the betrothal must be made.

And so she passed from the watchmen's presence and followed their directions, and soon she was clasping the feet of her beloved. There was no reserve now, no desire to have him withdraw to the mountains of Bethor or separation. There was only the clinging embrace that would never again let him go. There came the uncompromising welcome that brought him to her mother and to the most sacred chambers of her house, where the fondest place was given to him, and his dearness and nearness were recognized without reservation. Yes, even the mother's place to which, perhaps, she had clung until now, is now abandoned to a dearer and nearer.

Friend, thus you can seek the Lord. "For everyone who asks receives; he who seeks finds; and to him who knocks, the door will be opened" (Matthew 7:8). Very blessed it is to open immediately when He knocks, but blessed is it also to knock until He opens. So, seeking one,

> Come thy way to Zion's gate,
>   There till mercy lets thee in,
> Knock and seek and watch and wait.
>
> Knock. He knows the sinner's cry,
>   Weep. He loves the sinner's tear.
> Watch, for heavenly love is nigh.
>   Wait till heavenly light appear.

And when we find Him we must give Him the inmost chamber, the fondest love, the place that the dearest has held. It is when the sacrifice of the tenderest of earthly ties has been fully made that Christ becomes our All in all, and every earthly tie becomes more sacred and more true. The spirit of self-sacrifice is the secret of the truest happiness.

Once in India a company of soldiers were in extreme poverty and distress. The general entered a heathen temple. The natives besought him to spare their idols and warned him that if he touched a certain chief deity that every calamity would fall upon him and his troops. But he boldly marched up to the proud idol and striking it from its pedestal, he dashed it to pieces on the temple floor. To his astonishment and the surprise of the witnessing multitudes, countless treasures of silver and gold poured from its shattered core. It had been the storehouse for centuries of the treasures of kings, and all that it needed was to be shattered in order to enrich the needy whose hand had dared to strike the blow.

Friend, many of our idols stand between us and the wealth of God's infinite love and grace. Let us not fear to strike the fatal blow, and lo from the bosom of that which we perhaps spare as an Agag or cherish with an unholy clinging will come forth the wealth of infinite blessing and everlasting love.

CHAPTER 4

Wedding Days

"In that day," declares the LORD, "you will call me 'my husband'; you will no longer call me 'my master.' " (Hosea 2:16)

This beautiful section of the Song of Songs describes the wedding scene in the old oriental poem. It begins with a picture of the marriage procession coming up from the wilderness, the former home of the bride, amid clouds of fragrance, which look like pillars of smoke in the distance. She is borne in the litter or palanquin of King Solomon and is guarded by a band of 60 valiant men who march before and behind the royal bride to protect her from danger and "fear in the night." She is met by the king in a chariot of silver and gold, lined with costly tapestries presented by the daughters of Jerusalem as a gift of love. The royal bridegroom is crowned with a diadem of beauty and glory presented by his mother's loving hands.

The marriage procession fades into the meeting of the bridegroom and the bride. We next listen to his greeting of Shulamith and his words of admiration as he welcomes her with love and praise (Song of Songs 4:1-16). Then he leaves her for the remainder of the day until the evening shadows flee away, when he will come again, after all the marriage preparations are complete, to claim her as his bride and to take part in the wedding ceremonies and the wedding feast. Returning in the evening he greets her with words of still stronger admiration and love: "All beautiful you are, my darling; there is no flaw in you" (4:7). And then he pleads with her to turn her thoughts away from Lebanon, her old home, and turn her eye with single purpose and thought to him alone. He now calls her for the first time his spouse. The remaining verses of chapter 4 are the outpourings of his full heart, as he loves to dwell on the sweetness of her who has satisfied his soul's deepest love. All the most exquisite imagery of an oriental land is laid under tribute to praise the beauty and sweetness of the bride. The sweetness of the honeycomb, the exhilarance of wine, the smell of costly ointments, the rich fragrance of Lebanon, the beauty of the garden, the freshness of the fountains, the fruitfulness of the pomegranate, the manifold variety and delicacy of the perfumes of camphor, saffron, calamus, cinnamon, frankincense, myrrh, aloes and all the chief spices—all these pale before the sweetness of her love.

At length we hear her response (4:16). She turns all her being to his love and calls upon the north wind and the south wind to blow upon her garden that its spices may flow out. Then she invites her beloved to come into her garden and accept it as his own.

The scene closes with the bridegroom's response to her as he accepts her offered gift of herself. Then, the invited guests and friends bid them welcome to the marriage feast, "Eat, O friends, and drink; drink your fill, O lovers" (5:1).

Our Union with Christ

The great spiritual truth which all this oriental imagery covers is our union with the Lord Jesus Christ, the true Bridegroom of the church and of the heart. First we see the coming of the bride to meet the bridegroom. She comes up from the wilderness. It is there that Christ always calls His Bride.

> I am now going to allure her;
>> I will lead her into the desert
>> and speak tenderly to her.
> There I will give her back her vineyards,
>> and will make the Valley of Achor a door
>>> of hope.
> There she will sing as in the days of her
>>> youth. . . .
> "In that day," declares the LORD,
>> "[she] will call me 'my husband.' "
>>> (Hosea 2:14-16)

It is usually out of the deep, dark, lonely place of trial that we come into our deepest intimacy with Jesus and know the fullness of His love.

The pillars of smoke amid which she came are figures of the sweet fragrance of the heart, the incense of love, the one offering which makes the most unworthy and insignificant acceptable to the remembrance of love. This is all the bride has to bring—her love. But it is so deep and rich and sweet that it fills all the air with clouds of fragrance and pillars of smoke.

Once in the desert a wandering Arab found a spring. The water was so delicious that he could not keep it to himself, but filling a leather flask he bore it across the desert a hundred miles in the hot sun and sand, and presented it to his chief as an offering of his love. The water was all corrupted before it reached the prince, and when he tasted it it had no sweetness. But he betrayed no sign of its unpleasantness and thanked the kind bestower and sent him back laden with honors. His princes afterwards tasted the water, curious to know what strange charm it possessed, but to them it was loathsome. They looked with astonishment and disgust at their chief. "Oh," he said, "it had for me a taste which you could not discern. It was the taste of love. The kindness of heart that brought it was all that I could see. And I would not for the world have let him know that his gift itself was so worthless, because the love that brought it made it of infinite value."

Friend, we may be poor and unworthy, but if we bring to Jesus a heart of love, it will be to Him a priceless treasure of surpassing intrinsic values.

In the wedded life there can be no substitute for love. Without it marriage is a hideous mockery. And in Christian life and our relationship with Jesus Christ, without love we are but "a resounding gong or a clanging cymbal" (1 Corinthians 13:1). All our theories, ceremonies and religious forms are an offensive sham. And all that we may do, or think, or say, His sentence can only be, "You have forsaken your first love" (Revelation 2:4). "Because you are lukewarm . . . I am about to spit you out of my mouth" (3:16).

The Bride's Chariot

Next we see the chariot of the bride. It was furnished by her husband and defended by his own bodyguard. And so, as we come into our place of chosen intimacy with Jesus Christ, it is He Himself who bears us into this higher plane. The very love that brings us to His bosom is His own heavenly gift. The very power to rise to meet Him in this wondrous union is from Him. He bears us to His palace and to His heart in His own chariot. The Holy Spirit will teach us the wondrous secret of heavenly love, and often we will say, like the bride a little later, "Before I realized it, my desire set me among the royal chariots of my people" (Song of Songs 6:12).

The guards around the chariot that bore her to her beloved suggest to us the perils that surround us as we walk in the closer places of Christian experience. There is no place so full of peril as that which lies nearest to the gates of heaven and to the arms of Jesus. The fallen spirits of the air, the emissaries of Lucifer, son of the morning, are not only spirits of light but spirits of love. And there is a false love that would lower us to the depths of ruin as well as a true love that would lift us to the heights of heaven. Many a heart has been beguiled and seduced by lying spirits to a kind of love that is not the love life of the Lord. And by yielding to some delusive charm that claimed to be from heaven, the soul can lose its purity, and instead of becoming the bride of the Lamb become an unholy partner of Satanic power.

Thus, alas, the once pure church of apostolic days became the harlot of the great apostasy, and that which was so terribly fulfilled in the church has often been made as real in the individual life. This is the day, especially, when spiritualism, spiritism, theosophy, science falsely so called, and morbid sentimentalism, under the guise of leadings of the spirit, are betraying many hearts into the sad and sinful counterfeit of the love life of the Lord. But through God the heart that is wholly His will be guarded by His almighty hand, and the chariot of heavenly love will be defended by the armed hosts of His power and holiness. Let us keep our eye singly upon Him, our heart wholly true to Him. Let us not fear to draw near, for His guardian presence and heavenly panoply will protect us even from the wiles of the devil. And we will walk in the narrow paths of the heavenly life safe from all danger and fear even in the night. His jealous and mighty love will guard us like a chaste virgin from even the breath of defilement.

The Bridegroom Meeting His Bride

We see in this picture the coming of the bridegroom to meet his bride. he, too, has a chariot of silver and gold and royal purple, the gift of the daughters of Jerusalem. As he meets his bride, his head is crowned with the crown of love, and his heart is full of gladness in the day of his espousals.

Our beloved Lord would have us understand that His heart is as glad as ours in the consummation of His union with us. He has chosen us as the object of His peculiar and eternal love, and He needs our love as we need His. We may not be able to understand why one so much above us can be satisfied with the affection of those so unworthy of Him, but there is always something in love that is inexplicable. It has no reason but itself. He has loved us just because He has loved us, in a measure altogether out of proportion to any claim or fitness in the objects of that love. We contribute to His joy as well as to our own when we yield our hearts to our best Friend. Surely He has a right to claim from us the return which His love deserves. He has given up all else; this is His only portion. Let us not rob Him of any part of it.

The Bridegroom's Welcome to His Bride

His first words are a tribute to her loveliness, ending with the unqualified words of praise, "All beautiful you are, my darling; there is no flaw in you" (4:7). This is high praise to give, but it is the praise He longs to give to every one of His sanctified ones. It is not too high for the blood of Christ to cover. The soul that is washed in that fountain and robed in His spotless garments is whiter than the snow and spotless as Christ Himself. It is not that our personal character is perfect, but passing out of ourselves into Him and filled with Him, we are indeed able to claim even His own mighty assurance, "You are already clean because of the word I have spoken to you" (John 15:3).

Let us dare to believe it on the authority of His Word. We will please Him far better than when we are continually holding up the spots of our own unworthiness and betraying before His gaze the wretched corpses that He would have us bury forever out of sight.

The Focus of Her Gaze

Next, there comes a call to detach her thoughts and her affections altogether from former objects of attraction and fix her single eye on Him alone. "Come with me from Lebanon, my bride" (Song of Songs 4:8). That is, withdraw your thoughts from your old home, Lebanon, from the fair scenes of your childhood, from the tender associations of the past, from the beautiful Amana and Shenir. Forget your relatives and your father's house, and let your thoughts be all mine. This is His call to us to let every other interest and affection be concentrated in His great love. When we do this, then alone will we satisfy His heart. God's love is jealous for our own good as well as for His own glory, and He cannot accept a divided heart in a bond so dear as that of marriage.

His delight is her singleness of eye and heart. "You have stolen my heart with one glance of your eyes" (4:9). She has responded to his appeal; she has given him all her heart. She has dropped the far-off look from her longing gaze, and every thought and affection are centered in Him alone. The beautiful words which He uses in the parallel picture in Hosea are true of her. "You are to live with me . . . and I will live with you" (3:3). This is the secret of a consecrated and happy life, and the only life that can satisfy our Lord. Friend, has He got all your eye and all your heart?

His Higher Tribute

Next comes his higher tribute to her sweetness and love. He compares her in the closing verse of the chapter to the fountains, fruits and fragrance of an oriental garden. "You are a garden locked up, my sister, my bride" (Song of Songs 4:12). It is the enclosure of the garden which constitutes the secret of its value. It is not open to the trampling feet of all the wild creatures of the woods, but it is enclosed for Him alone and guarded from the desecrating tread of others. This is the reason why our blessings so often fade away or leak out as from open vessels.

We are not enclosed, but like a garden open to the wild beasts of the field and the destroying, desecrating tramp of every unclean thing. We receive a blessing in the house or at the altar of prayer. But often before an hour has past we have lost it and wonder why. The reason is very plain. Some idle talker has talked it all away, some vain and volatile flood of thoughts and imaginations has taken possession of our heart, and lo! the Holy Dove, disgusted, has taken His flight. Some wretched, miserable, idle conversation or unholy gossip has been permitted to occupy our attention, the garden gate has been opened and lo, the flowers and fruits are trodden down by unholy feet or devoured by rapacious mouths. Our God will not abide in company with Belial. If we would know the joy of the Lord and have our Beloved dwell with us, we must enclose our garden in the walls of holy separation. "Come out from them and be separate. . . . Touch no unclean thing, and [He] will receive [us] . . . and [we] will be [His] sons and daughters" (2 Corinthians 6:17-18), the Bride of His exclusive affection.

The same thought is expressed by the fountain sealed, the spring shut up. It is the picture of a heart separated unto God. It is the compression of the spring that gives it its impelling power and sends the waters high up sometimes in their heavenward flow and keeps them ever fresh and pure. The narrower the torrent's channel, the mightier its rush of waters. The broad stream becomes a stagnant swamp. Likewise, the heart that has room for all promiscuous things ceases to have any deep love for anything, and Christ will not accept its mixtures and compromises. "Because he loves me," He says of the single heart, "I will rescue him" (Psalm 91:14). "Delight yourself in the LORD and he will give you the desires of your heart" (37:4).

The Garden's Fruitfulness

Next we have the fruitfulness of the garden: "Your plants are an orchard of pomegranates with choice fruits" (Song of Songs 4:13). It is singular that the pomegranate should be the only fruit specified. If you ever examined one you may see the reason. Cut this singular-looking fruit through the center and look at a section of it as it is exposed by the knife. Your attention will be at once attracted, not to the rich color of the fruit, or even to its delicious perfume or taste, but, above everything else, to its countless seeds. It is one mass of little germs, there being enough in a single pomegranate to multiply it a thousandfold.

The fruit which God wants from His children is fruit that reproduces itself in other souls. The grace that has saved us can just as well save the world. The blessing that we have received can be multiplied by all the people who are willing to accept it. God wants each of us to be a seed which will spring forth and bear fruit, if not as much as the pomegranate, at least "multiplying thirty, sixty or even a hundred times" (Mark 4:8). Our salvation is not a selfish luxury, but a sacred trust. Our every new experience is given us for some other more than for ourselves. All that God does for us is intended by Him to be reflected and transmitted through our lives, so that on account of us "the desert and the parched land will be glad; the wilderness will rejoice and blossom" (Isaiah 35:1). Friend, is our Master able to delight in us as in His Bride because of our fruitfulness? Is our life repeating itself, not by hard effort but by spontaneous and springing life?

The Garden's Fragrance

But there is something far higher than fruit, and so the next characteristic of the Lord's garden, and the one that is emphasized in sevenfold variety and fullness, is fragrance. No less than seven different kinds of spices are mentioned in the verses that follow. Some of them are familiar to us; others are less known, but all express the idea of sweetness, of the devotion of love, of the inexpressible atmosphere of heavenliness. The perfume is the soul of the plant. It expresses the finer, the more delicate essence of its life. It stands for that in our Christian experience and in the outgoing of our heart, which is divinest, most sensitive, spiritual and devout. It is the very aroma of the heart, and it is in this that our beloved Lord most delights, and by this that the hearts of men are to be most deeply touched.

Some of the spices mentioned here are quite suggestive. The aloe was a bitter spice. It tells of the sweetness of bitter things, the bittersweet, which has its own fine application that only those can understand who have felt it. The myrrh was used to embalm the dead, and it tells of death to something. It is the sweetness which comes to the heart after it has died to its self-will and pride and sin. Oh, the inexpressible charm that hovers about some lives simply because they bear upon their chastened countenance and mellow spirit the impress of the cross. They bear the holy evidence of having died to something that was once proud and strong but is now forever at the feet of Jesus in His bottomless tomb. They are far sweeter for having had it and died to it than if they never had possessed the proud will and died to the strong desire. It is the heavenly charm of a broken spirit and a contrite heart, the music that springs from the minor key, the sweetness that comes from the touch of the frost upon the ripened fruit.

The frankincense was a fragrance that came from the touch of the fire. It was the burning powder that rose in clouds of sweetness from the bosom of the flames. It tells of the heart whose sweetness has been called forth, perhaps by the flames of affliction, perhaps by the baptism of the Holy Spirit. It is the heavenly fire that kindles all the heart until the holy place of the soul is filled with clouds of praise and prayer. Friend, are you giving out the spices, the perfumes, the sweet odors of the heart so that even as the traveler is conscious the moment he enters the waters of the orient that he is near the land of the sun, and even as Milton sings,

> Far off at sea the soft winds blow
> Sabaean odors from the spicy shores of Araby the blest.

The Bride's Response

"Awake, north wind, and come, south wind! Blow on my garden, that its fragrance may spread abroad. Let my lover come into his garden and taste its choice fruits" (Song of Songs 4:16).

This is the surrender of the bride to her beloved. It comes with all the treasures of her affection and her life, and, at the same time, the acknowledgment of her dependence upon a higher power to evoke the sweetness that was slumbering in her being. Not even all the spices that he had named could send out their perfume until his own breath first blew upon them. It is the cry of dependence upon the Holy Spirit for every new breath of love or praise. We have not in our hearts a crystallized and stereotyped sweetness which is at our command. We are simply the strings of an aeolian harp, dead and silent unless breathed upon from above, and every motion or aspiration of piety, or prayer, or praise must be awakened afresh by the breath of God Himself.

It is blessed to know that He does not expect us to even think a thought of ourselves. He is ready if we are but surrendered to Him, to blow upon our yielded hearts and awaken all the chords of melody. Or, to change the figure, to call forth all the breathings of heavenly love. He is both the north wind and the south wind. He is the north wind that sharpens, braces, reproves, withers—even, if need be, frosts sometimes with its cutting breath and sweeps away the chaff, the rubbish and the withered leaves. And He is the south wind that comes with healing, with consolation, with sweet encouragement, with tender sympathy, with heavenly hope, with all the tenderness of brooding love. He knows how to adapt Himself to each of our changing moods and needs. The heart that is fully yielded to Him will accept either as He sends them and praise Him alike for both.

Thus we see in her response the beautiful spirit of devotion to him in all the rich fruition of her being. Her garden was for her beloved and for none but him. She did not wish to be sweet that others might see her sweetness, but that he might be satisfied. Oh, it is blessed and beautiful to shine for Christ alone. It is blessed to be lovely just so He may be glad, to pour rich ointment on His head and feet, to serve not the church or the people, but the Lord. It is blessed to have Him say of everything we do, even for others, "You did it for Me."

Friend, is your garden all for Him? Is your love for Him, your prayer for Him, your sacrifice for Him? Is your recompense enough if He is pleased and if He approves? Is your motto, "For to me, to live is Christ" (Philippians 1:21), "so that now as always Christ will be exalted in my body, whether by life or by death" (1:20).

The Bridegroom's Acceptance

Finally there comes the bridegroom's acceptance of her love and his generous invitation to the wedding guests. "I have come into my garden, my sister, my bride; I have gathered my myrrh with my spice. I have eaten my honeycomb and my honey; I have drunk my wine and my milk. Eat, O friends, and drink; drink your fill, O lovers" (Song of Songs 5:1).

We do not realize enough how much of our service is due to Christ Himself and how truly He appreciates and enjoys the riches of our affection. He accepts the surrender we make. He feeds upon the banquet we spread. He sups with us and enjoys as the recompense of the travail of His soul the little that we bring to Him. Then He gives it all to others, and nothing is so blessed to them as that which was first given to Christ. It is the heart that is wholly dedicated to Jesus' headship that fills all the house with its odor. None can be such blessings to the world as those who, beyond all they do for the world, love and serve the Lord alone.

It is when we come into the bosom of His love that we are able to stand, as the bride of the heavenly host at the gates of His palace, and invite His wandering children to the feast that His love has provided. "The Spirit and the bride say, 'Come!' "

(Revelation 22:17). It is not until we become the Bride, and are thus filled with the Spirit, and able to represent the Bridegroom that we can say, "Come" in all the fullness of effectual power—to so say it that he that is thirsty will come, and whosoever will, will take the water of life freely.

Friend, if we would be a perfect blessing to a sad and lost world, let us come and enter into the love life of the Lord.

CHAPTER 5

Testing Days

Who is this that appears like the dawn,
fair as the moon, bright as the sun,
majestic as the stars in procession?
(Song of Songs 6:10)

The structure of this section of the Song of Songs is very clear and simple. The marriage is over and the bride's first trial comes.

It is a very serious trial and the cause of it is chiefly her own folly. Lying asleep at night in her chamber, her bridegroom comes to the door, knocks upon it and speaks to her, requesting her to open and admit him. Half asleep and self-indulgent she reluctantly answers, "I have taken off my robe—must I put it on again? I have washed my feet—must I soil them again?" (5:3). But as he still lingers, she rises with fingers dripping with myrrh. Freshly anointing herself to receive him, she opens the door. But she is too late. Chilled by the delay, he has gone. She searches for him up and down the streets in the darkness, but in vain. She wanders, anxious and half-crazed, through the town in darkness, but she cannot find him. She meets the watchmen on her way and they treat her with rudeness and harshness. And the keepers of the walls insult her. Finally, heartbroken and disappointed, she cries to her maidens, "If you find my lover, . . . tell him I am faint with love" (5:8).

Then her maidens tempt her by asking her what is her beloved more than any other beloved. They perhaps insinuate that there are plenty of others just as good if she will only consent to let him go. It is then that her true nobility and fidelity shine out in spite of her mistake. Faithfully she answers, with words of love and devotion, that her beloved is the chief among 10,000 and altogether lovely. She explains that he is not only lovely, but true to her. Though she cannot find him, she persists in telling of her beloved and her devotion to him, summing it all up in the testimony, "I am my lover's and my lover is mine" (6:3).

Then it is that he rewards her faithful heart by suddenly appearing. He greets her with words of warmest admiration and boundless praise, calling her "beautiful . . . as Tirzah, lovely as Jerusalem, majestic as troops with banners" (6:4). Then her maidens join in the chorus of admiration and utter perhaps a little later in the drama, probably as she goes from her chamber in the morning, fresh with her loveliness. "Who is this that appears like the dawn, fair as the moon, bright as the sun, majestic as the stars in procession?" (6:10).

They beg her to dance for them the simple

dance of Mahanaim, and, as she grants their request, her lover breaks out again with ascriptions of praise. "How beautiful your sandaled feet, O prince's daughter!" (7:1). The scene closes with his fresh tribute of affection and admiration (7:1-9) and with her response of complete devotion, "I belong to my lover, and his desire is for me" (7:10).

The Spiritual Lessons

The spiritual lessons of all this part of the drama may be summed up as follows:

1. Her Lack of Prompt Obedience

Her immediate failure was a lack of prompt obedience to his call and this is ever sure to bring us sorrow, separation and loss. Paul reminds us that "they that are after the flesh do mind the things of the flesh; but they that are after the Spirit the things of the Spirit" (Romans 8:5, KJV). The closer we come to Christ, the more subject to His call we must be. Love is jealous and divine love wants us ever at its summons and quickly responsive to its faintest whisper. There is no greater word in the Christian's experience than the word *obey*. God has given His Spirit to them that obey Him (Acts 5:32). Christ has made the manifestation of His peculiar love dependent upon this very thing. "Whoever has my commands and obeys them, he is the one who loves me. He who loves me will be loved by my Father, and I too will love him and show myself to him" (John 14:21). The intimate and abiding communion of Jesus is wholly dependent upon our obedience and responsiveness to His voice.

The causes of the beloved woman's failure were indolence and self-indulgence. This was a great slight to her lord. She had preferred her comfort to his. She could lie in luxurious ease while he was standing outside the door, his head wet with the dew and his locks with the drops of the night. What a sad picture of a bridegroom and a bride! What a sad, sad symbol of the attitude of the Lord Jesus Christ with respect to the very church that He has redeemed and wedded to Himself. She in luxury and selfishness, and He out into the cold and the darkness. The spirits of indolence, languor and slothfulness are largely responsible for our frequent despondence, and therefore our Master has said, "If anyone would come after me, he must deny himself and take up his cross daily and follow me" (Luke 9:23).

It is true she responded at length and opened the door, but she did not do it promptly, and her obedience was too late. The same thing is not the same thing at different times. That which is done at once is twice done. The children of Israel were quite willing to enter the land of promise the day after the Lord summoned, but He would not go with them. In matters of mutual confidence, hesitation implies distrust or at least indifference, and it is fatal to the fine, delicate complexion of sensitive love. It is true she brought her hands full of myrrh and the door handle dripped with sweetness as she touched it, but that was poor substitute for the sweetness of the heart. Her myrrh was all lost for lack of prompt, obedient love. We may bring much to Christ as a substitute for love but it is all lost. Whatsoever He says to you, do it, and do it at once.

Friend, learn in the life of abiding to be quick and to recognize and respond to the Master's voice. Whether it is the call to prayer, or to stillness, or to service, or to sacrifice, let the heart quickly answer, "Yes."

I will say, Yes, to Jesus,
Whatever He commands,
I will run to do His bidding,
With loving heart and hands.

I will listen to hear His whispers,
And learn His will each day.
And always gladly answer, yea,
Whatever He may say.

2. Her Humiliation and Suffering

Next we look at the humiliation and suffering which follow her failure. The first sad consequence of her mistake was the loss of her bridegroom's presence and the slight and offense which he so deeply felt. He withdrew from her door and left her alone. There is no trial more deep and keen to a devout spirit than the loss of the Lord's presence. That which once we did not value is now become the very essence of our life and happiness. And the moment that prevailing presence is gone we are conscious of a void that nothing else can fill and an anguish of which none is more keen. There is a deep sense of Christ's wounded love and the Holy Spirit's withdrawal in grief and displeasure, and sometimes there is a deep and terrible dread upon the soul lest He may have taken His everlasting flight. "My God, my God, why have you forsaken me?" (Mark 15:34) is its bitter cry. "If only I knew where to find him; if only I could go to his dwelling!" (Job 23:3) is its perplexed, distracted question.

This is something quite different from the withdrawal of the Lord's manifestations. Those He may be often pleased to take from the soul with which He has no controversy, simply to try the faith and teach to trust Himself in the dark. But this is something deeper and keener. It is the Lord saying, "I will go and return unto My own place, until they acknowledge their iniquity" (See Jeremiah 3:6-13). There is a judicial severity in it which is meant to reprove the heart for its neglect and disobedience. It is a very keen and dreadful thing for a child of God to fall under the hand of its Father's chastening. But the reason is very plain. And it is necessary that we learn it thoroughly and never forget it, and that henceforth whenever He speaks to us we will instantly answer, "Yes."

3. Her Painful Seeking

The next sad consequence of her failure was the

long and painful seeking, and the cruel harshness of the watchmen whom she met on the street as she vainly sought her lord. It is strange how hard it is to find our way back again when we get far from God. That which once seemed so simple is now as dark as night. The promise that once seemed to glow with light is all full of darkness and gloom. The throne of grace at which we knelt, where heaven came down our souls to greet, is surrounded with clouds and thick darkness. The very conception of Christ seems dim, and God Himself distant and strange. The delightful sense of nearness is gone, and we do not know how to pray. We seem like one perplexed and distracted in the night, fluttering, bewildered, heartbroken.

Friend, you are not the poor soul away from the Lord that cried in the night, "If only I knew where to find him." Let the recollection of your misery be an everlasting restraint upon your heart. Abide ever near Him and quickly listen to His voice and obey His slightest call.

At such times others do not understand us. Even the very watchmen on Zion's walls seem lacking in tenderness and sympathy. They do not enter into our distress. They treat us with harshness. How often the very ministers of the gospel will say something trivial to some perplexed, troubled soul that has lost its consecration or is seeking for a deeper life. I myself have said in the earlier years of my ministry, "Oh, you are just a little melancholy and sentimental and nervous. All you want is a little fresh air or good company or medicine to get out of the blues, and cheer up, and give up dreaming." Often the unwise teacher will tempt the soul to abandon its notion of sanctification, to give the whole thing up as a delusion and come down to the ordinary plane of Christian life, and treat its former experience as a mistake. Sometimes the watchmen go further than this, and the erring one is treated with severity, rebuke and humiliation, rather than with tenderness, gentleness and helpfulness. Then the soul will turn away from all men, crying, like poor Job, "Miserable comforters are you all!" (Job 16:2). "I [will] appeal to God; I [will] lay my cause before him" (5:8).

Still further, she is not only harshly treated by the watchmen, but actually tempted by her own companions. "How is your beloved better than others?" (Song of Songs 5:9), they tauntingly ask. This is how the world comes to the lonely and aching heart. The world tries to make it think that earthly love and pleasure can heal its wound and satisfy the aching void. "You have lost your new joy, but there are joys just as sweet that you may have with us. Return to your old friendships and accept the world's smile." Oh, how alluring is that which she sometimes holds out to the aching heart. Sometimes but too successfully does she apply her flattering appeals and fascinating charms, and many, for a time at least, have sunk back into the arms of the world and lost their first love. There is no time that Satan and the world tempt the heart so persuasively as when it has lost the joy of the Lord. It is a very perilous thing to allow disobedience or despondency to betray us into the hands of our enemy, who is only too ready to take advantage of his opportunity. But thank God if at such an hour we can, like her, stand fully armed in the panoply of love and repel all the world's alluring appeals with the testimony of our faithfulness.

4. Her Final Temptation

There is yet one more subtle temptation which the adversary applies in the hour of the soul's desertion. "Where has your lover gone, most beautiful of women?" (6:1). This is the taunt of our scornful foe, who would insinuate a doubt of our Bridegroom's fidelity. "Has He left you? Is this the lover of whom you boasted so bravely? Has He deserted you so soon and left you to wander upon the streets in loneliness and humiliation? Is He after all not such a faithful lover as you thought? Perhaps you had better let Him go. Perhaps He has gone forever, and you had better stop searching for Him."

This was David's experience when he cried out,

My tears have been my food
    day and night,
while men say to me all day long,
    "Where is your God?" . . .
"Why must I go about mourning,
    oppressed by the enemy?"
My bones suffer mortal agony
    as my foes taunt me,

saying to me all day long,
  "Where is your God?"
        (Psalm 42:3, 9-10).

Oh, friend, keep out of the path of the backslider. It is beset with snares and thorns. If you do venture into it, "your backsliding will rebuke you. Consider then and realize how evil and bitter it is for you when you forsake the LORD your God" (Jeremiah 2:19). But if you have wandered do not be discouraged. Stand firm amid all the temptation, like the bride, as we will see. And when you are restored you will remember the experience as an everlasting warning, and will walk softly all your days closer to the side of your Beloved.

5. *Her Fidelity*

Next we see her fidelity through all the trials of her faith and love. First, she continued seeking. She did not go back to bed again and fall asleep in languid indifference. But the moment she found out her mistake she endeavored to correct it. She continued to search for her lord until she found him. So, friend, there is always this resource left you, "Ask and it will be given to you; seek and you will find; knock and the door will be opened to you" (Matthew 7:7). It is as true for the backslider as it is for the sinner. "You will seek me and find me when you seek me with all your heart" (Jeremiah 29:13).

Next, she not only searched but she continued steadfast in her love. Her one continual testimony, when they asked her what her beloved was more than any other beloved, was that he was "radiant and ruddy, outstanding among ten thousand" (Song of Songs 5:10). Not for a moment would she depreciate his charms or yield to a disparagement of his worth, but she boldly testified to his grace and beauty in the midst of all her trials. And, in the face of all her temptresses, her true and loving heart was immovable as a rock from its steadfast affection. All the world could not tempt her to even a thought of disloyalty or compromise. So, friend, even if you have lost the joy of your purpose, the loyalty of your love, cry, "Though I see Him not, yet I love Him. Though I have sinned against Him, yet He knows that I love Him. Though I have been foolish and forgetful, yet my heart is true. And, though all the world should tempt me, He and He alone will be my Beloved. Though I never see His face again, or hear His voice, yet I will be true to Him in life and death forevermore."

Therefore she was not only steadfast in her devotion, but she retained her faith in his love to her with unfaltering confidence. And when they seemed to imply that he had deserted her, she still declared, "I am my beloved's, and my beloved is mine. He is as true to me as I am to him, and, although he hides his face for a little, his heart, I know, has never changed. Though He forsake me, I will cling to him; though he slay me, I will trust him" (author's paraphrase). Dear friend, is this your attitude even in the darkness?

"Who among you fears the LORD and obeys the word of his servant? Let him who walks in the dark, who has no light, trust in the name of the LORD" (Isaiah 50:10).

Her Beloved's Appearing

Finally her lover appears. Suddenly he stands before her. He has heard her loving testimony. His heart has been moved with tenderness for all her trials. And she is dearer to him than ever as he sees her steadfast purpose, amid all the testing ordeal, to be his and his alone. So he rewards her faithfulness. "You are beautiful, my darling, as Tirzah, lovely as Jerusalem, majestic as troops with banners. . . . My dove, my perfect one" (Song of Songs 6:4, 9).

It is Christ's admiring testimony to the heart that stands true to Him through all the fiery trial. The old promise was ever fulfilled. "Put your hope in God, for I will yet praise him, my Savior and my God" (Psalm 42:11).

Brighter than His first appearing, dearer than even the soul's first love, is the hour when He comes again to the desolate and wandering heart. "To me this is like the days of Noah," He cries, as He renews His covenant, "when I swore that the waters of Noah would never again cover the earth. So now I have sworn not to be angry with you, never to rebuke you again" (Isaiah 54:9). " 'For a brief moment I abandoned you, but with deep compassion I will bring you back. In a surge of anger I hid my face from you for a moment, but with everlasting kindness I will have compassion

on you,' says the LORD your Redeemer" (54:7-8).
Oh, the joy of the restored heart when the Lord
arises with healing in His wings, and the long
night of waiting ends in a morning of joy.

Her New Appearance

Finally we see her new loveliness after her trials
are over. "Who is this that appears like the dawn,
fair as the moon, bright as the sun, majestic as the
stars in procession?" (Song of Songs 6:10) her
maidens ask, as they behold her happiness the
morning after her bridegroom has returned. The
last shadow of her sorrow has passed away, her
face is bright as the morning and fresh as the
morning dew. Her beauty is fair as the moon, and
its luster has remained all through the night of
sorrow. Her faith and love are glorious as the sun,
and the strength of her character has come forth
from the testing armed for all coming conflicts
even as an army with banners.

1. The Morning

The morning is especially the type of freshness. It speaks of a Christian life that is ever
new, a buoyant spirit that ever springs with
spontaneous life and fullness, like the springing
dawn and the fresh zest which starts forth upon
a new day with the complete oblivion of yester-
day's toil and care.

2. The Moon

The moon is the beautiful figure of the light

that shines in the darkness. It tells of the faith and love that live on in unclouded clearness even through the dark shades of the night. The sun tells of the stronger light for the service of the day, for endurance and trial are not the main business of life. It is a precious discipline to fit us for more strong and positive service. But the strong, clear light of the day is higher, even as the sunlight is better than moonlight. And after we have stood the test of the night and shone with the pure radiance of the moon, God sends us forth into the daylight and sunlight of service. There He expects us to shed this strong light upon all around us and go forth in it ourselves to the work to which He calls us.

3. The Stars

The last figure, "the stars in procession," or as the King James puts it, "an army with banners," tells of the strength that comes from the discipline of trial, the courage of faith, the precious, priceless lessons which fit us for the conflicts that lie before us. God wants us to be not only sweet, but strong; not only to be the joy of His heart, but a terror to the enemy of our souls and of His kingdom. It is not until we have fought that enemy in our own hearts that we are prepared to go forth in aggressive conflict and stand against him in the souls of others and the work of the gospel. It was after Christ had stayed 40 days in the wilderness that He went forth in the power of the Spirit into Galilee and came out guiltless and triumphant over all the powers of darkness.

The Divine Purpose

This is the divine purpose of our testings. "These [trials] have come so that your faith—of greater worth than gold, which perishes even though refined by fire—may be proved genuine and may result in praise, glory and honor when Jesus Christ is revealed" (1 Peter 1:7). "No discipline seems pleasant at the time, but painful. Later on, however, it produces a harvest of righteousness and peace for those who have been trained by it" (Hebrews 12:11). "And the God of all grace, who called you to his eternal glory in Christ, after you have suffered a little while, will himself restore you and make you strong, firm and steadfast. To him be the power for ever and ever. Amen" (1 Peter 5:10-11).

Friend, is this the effect of your testings? Are they bringing into your life the freshness of the morning, the quiet light of the moon which shines on through the dark night, the clear light of day that fits you for the service and duties of your life, the settled strength and established purpose which enables you to withstand in the evil day, and to go forth in the strength of God in aggressive warfare against the devil and all his legions?

The Deeper Love

This is the deeper love into which her trials have brought her. There is a very beautiful order running through her testimonies regarding her love. Her first testimony is, "My lover is mine and I am his" (Song of Songs 2:16). This gives no prominence to his love for her, and there is, if possible, a little touch of selfishness in the thought of him as her first glad consciousness. A little later her testimony is, "I am my lover's and my lover is mine" (6:3). This speaks of a change in her attitude and thought. Her love to him and her entire surrender is the more prominent thought.

But there is a third expression, a little later, after the return of his presence. It is simply this, "I belong to my lover" (7:10). Every trace of selfishness in her love is gone, and her whole being is absorbed with the simple consciousness of being all his own. This is the crowning blessing of her trial. It brings her into a complete surrender and wholehearted devotion to him with her one concern to please him, to satisfy him, to glorify him, and even the enjoyment of him is lost in the thought of his enjoyment of her and delight in her. Surely sorrow has been crowned with infinite and eternal glory, and trial has been found unto praise and honor and glory in her happy experience. So may each of us stand in the hour of testing and find through our fiery trials a far more exceeding and eternal weight of glory.

CHAPTER 6

Home Longings

*Come away, my lover, and be like a gazelle or like
a young stag on the spice-laden mountains.*
(Song of Songs 8:14)

"Yes, I am coming soon." Amen. Come, Lord Jesus.
(Revelation 22:20)

This last text is the interpreter of the first. Both
express, one in figure and the other in simple
prose, the longing of every true Christian heart for
the coming of our Lord. How different the closing
cry of the Song of Songs from the bride's earlier
song in the second chapter! There it is, "Turn, my
lover, and be like a gazelle or like a young stag on
the rugged hills" (Song of Songs 2:17), rugged
hills meaning "division." But here it is, "Come
away, my lover, and be like a gazelle or like a
young stag on the spice-laden mountains" or the
mountains of love, for the spices suggested by the
Hebrew word just mean the "fragrance of love."

We have already seen that the bride became
weary of the constant distractions of the life that

she was living in the great city. She longed to return to her early home where she could have her
beloved all to herself, and, in the simplicity of
their home life, could meet him without restraint
or thought of the keen eyes of a conventional
world. This is expressive of the longing of the
church for the Lord's second coming, and the instinctive cry of every holy heart, "Come, Lord Jesus, come quickly." Let us endeavor to understand
the true spirit and limitations of this desire. What
is a true scriptural home longing?

Not Morbid Discontent

We do not mean by this a morbid discontent
with life, either from the *ennui* of satiety with pleasure or business, or from the deeper despair that
comes from trouble, and which so often hurls the
discouraged heart into reckless or cowardly suicide.
There may be a deep weariness with life which is
entirely wrong and even utterly cowardly and
mean. The spectacle of Elijah lying under the juni-
per tree and crying, "I have had enough, LORD. . . .
Take my life; I am no better than my ancestors" (1
Kings 19:4), and Jonah sitting under his withered
gourd and asking Jehovah to take away his life because Nineveh had been spared and his reputation
as a prophet had suffered loss, are but samples of
many kinds of discontent and morbidness that may
always be found among the generations of earth.
But this is far from the spirit to which our subject
applies. Disappointed affection, unsuccessful business, the bitter consequences of our own mistakes

and misdeeds, the reaction of wild and reckless passion, the terrors of a guilty conscience or the hard and oppressive circumstances of life—all these may lead one to cry out like poor Job, "I despise my life; I would not live forever" (Job 7:16). But it is often the most selfish and unmanly thing that a man can do, to run away from his difficulties and leave his helpless family and friends to stem the tide that he was not brave enough to meet. There may be a milder desire for death, one that does not lead to reckless suicide, but which is at the best only a longing to get free from suffering and which has in it no real devotion or spirituality. Let us not be deceived by the counterfeit and palm off mere jaded languor as heavenly mindedness.

There is a true longing to be with Christ, which we find expressed all through the pages of the Scriptures and the utterances of all true Christian biography. There is a ripening of the grain which makes the heads hang low and the fruit mellow and ready to fall. There is a true and beautiful sense in which the apostle can say, "I desire to depart and be with Christ, which is better by far; but it is more necessary for you that I remain in the body" (Philippians 1:23-24). Here we find a sound and wholesome readiness and even gladness to be with the Lord in a better world. Yet there is not a tinge of morbidness about it, but rather, on the contrary, a bright and radiant heartiness and hopefulness. There is a real preference to remain amid the toil and conflict of life for the sake of others and for the Master's work. But under all this there is a heart springing heavenward, a spirit that often longs for the rest and communion of the life beyond, and, like a caged bird, poises its wings for a higher and everlasting flight. Such heavenly aspirations breathe through God's holy Word and the hymnology of the ages as well as the highest experiences of the best of saints. Yet even this does not express the meaning of our text, and the most scriptural form of the saints' "longing for home."

A Longing for the Second Coming

It is not so much a desire for even heaven as a definite longing for the personal coming of the Lord Jesus Christ, and the setting up of the kingdom which His advent is to bring. This is very definitely expressed by the apostle in the fifth chapter of Second Corinthians, where he distinguishes the expectation of death very clearly from the expectation of the Lord's coming and the resurrection. "We do not wish to be unclothed," he says, referring to death, "but to be clothed with our heavenly dwelling," meaning the resurrection, "so that what is mortal may be swallowed up by life" (5:4). This is the Christian's true hope—the Lord's personal return, and the life immortal which this will bring to the body as it rises in His glorious likeness, and death is swallowed up by life immortal.

This is a very different thing from the expectation of death. There is a most erroneous impression abroad among many Christians with respect to the Lord's coming. When He bids us to always be ready, ever ready, He certainly does not mean that we are to be continually looking for death. He means that we are to be looking and hastening for the coming of our Lord. We are to prepare to meet Him when He descends from the skies to claim His bride and to reward His servants. This is a very different thing from the expectation of death. That is a looking down into the tomb. This is a looking up into the air. That is a depressing thought. This is a living and comforting one. Nowhere do we find our Master bidding us keep our eyes upon the tomb. But often He admonishes us to watch for His return and to stand with loins girded and lights burning, like men that wait for their Lord when He will return from the wedding. Such a desire and expectation is not only scriptural, but most sanctifying and quickening. It will lead to personal holiness and faithfulness in the discharge of our ministry and duties. It is an incentive to separation from the world such as nothing else can afford. It will give a nobility to life and shed the halo of its glory over all its work and all our way. It will inspire us like a pole star to lofty aspirations and to the highest and noblest sacrifices and service. There are abundant reasons why our heart should feel this heavenly desire.

Not Our Resting Place

The world is not fitted to be our rest. It is too small for a heart that has felt the enlarging of God's indwelling presence. It is too sad for the development of our heaven-born joy. There is no longing in the human heart so pure and sweet as the longing for home. Yet how few homes there are on earth that reach the highest ideal of even man's thought, and none of these are exempt from the touch of that hand which falls most heavily of all on the sweetest and happiest shrines. It is where love has been most sweet and heavenly, and happiness most divine, that the parting which death at last brings is most keenly felt. The very depth of our joy only intensifies the measure of our pain, so that the heart cries amid the wreck of earth's sweetest home circles,

> Friend after friend departs,
> Who hath not lost a friend?
> There is no union here of hearts
> That finds not here an end.
> Were this trial world our only rest,
> Living or dying, none were best.

The heart that is born from above instinctively reaches upward and rises heavenward, even as the river flows to the ocean and fire ascending seeks the sun.

The Unspeakable Blessings

The coming of the blessed Lord may well be an object of desire because of the unspeakable blessings which it is going to bring us. Not only will it take away from us a thousand sources of sorrow and pain, but it will bring to us the perfection of our own being. All that we know of holiness here will reach its maturity there and rise to a manhood to which all our present experiences are but as the play toys of an infant. Our physical life will reach its completeness there in the resurrection power and glory which will exalt us above the limitations of space and matter and thrill our being with a fullness of life like His own.

It will bring still greater blessing to the world. It will be the time of the restitution of all things of which the prophets have spoken since the beginning of the world. It will bring to this sad and sin-cursed earth more than paradise restored. For a thousand happy years the world will become the theater of the highest and divinest possibilities of God's power and grace. Then the philanthropist will see his dreams of human happiness fulfilled. Then our wretched political systems will give place to a reign of beneficence and happiness, and generation after generation rejoice in finding at last all that freedom and righteousness really mean.

David Livingstone will look upon the continent for which he died, smiling in the loveliness of millennial righteousness. John Williams will wander through the lovely islands of Polynesia, where he shed his blood, and see every drop transformed into rubies of eternal glory and recompense in scenes as holy as they are fair. John Howard will seek in vain for a prison beneath the sun and recall with rapture the prayers and tears that he spent amid these gloomy scenes of human misery. William Wilberforce will gaze with wonder and delight upon a globe where it will be impossible to find a fetter or a slave. Frances Willard will search for a thousand years before she will find a drunkard in the streets of the New Jerusalem. It is doubtful if even the fairest of our earthly scenes, our cemeteries, will be found. At least even death, if it comes at all during that age, will be robbed of its sting and will probably be but a transformation from the lower to the higher plane, from the natural to the resurrection life. Oh, for the sake of a groaning world, may we not well cry,

> Oh, long-expected day, begin,
> Dawn on this scene of pain and sin.

The Savior Will Be Visible

But the best of all reasons for desiring this blessed homecoming is that it is to bring us our Savior in visible, continual and perfect fellowship forevermore. The joy of the bride is the bridegroom; the hope of His coming is centered in Himself. In this beautiful poem the reason the bride longs to be back at her home is not so much to see her mother or her garden as to be able to be ever with her beloved.

"If only you were to me like a brother," she cries. "Then, if I found you outside, I would kiss you, and no one would despise me. I would lead you and bring you to my mother's house—she who has taught me. . . . His left arm is under my head and his right arm embraces me" (Song of Songs 8:1-3).

This is also the secret of the Christian's longing. It is to be with Christ which makes it far better to depart. The Lamb is the light of the city above, and the Lord is its glory. It will bring Christ Himself. It is true we have Him now, but not as we will then. We will see His face. We will dwell continually in His glorious presence. We will behold His beauty. We will commune with Him without restraint. We will see the grandeur of His kingdom and be partners with Him in the government of the millennial world. We will be glad in His joy, as we will see forever the glorious fruition of all His sorrow and the eternal results of redemption in the ages to come.

In this beautiful song the bride speaks not only of the joys that wait for her at home, but the joys she has laid up for him. "At our door is every delicacy, both new and old, that I have stored up for you, my lover" (7:13). We think of what that day will mean for us, but do we think of what it will mean for Him, as He gazes upon the innumerable souls that have been saved and glorified through His sufferings and love? As each of them brings his crowns and his rewards and lays them at His blessed feet, oh, the joy that will swell His noble heart as He gazes upon that spectacle of happiness and eternal transformation, and feels that one of those shining ones would be worth all the cost of Calvary. Have we something laid up for that day? Are we converting our treasures, our friendships, our affections into eternal memorials that some day we can bring to Him as the wedding gift of that glorious day?

Our Loved Ones

It will bring us our loved ones. When He comes again, they also that sleep in Jesus will God bring with Him. It will give us back our dead. As the years go, how the friends of the past diminish. How the friends of the future increase. The other day I was talking with a dear old saint who desired to commit to someone the administration of an important trust after he had passed away, but he could think of no one to whom he would commit it. They were all gone, and he stood alone. This is not his home, but oh, how thickly they are clustering at yonder gates. What troops will meet us as we enter there—brothers, sisters, children, husbands, wives. Oh, how memory teems with them, and hope lights up that looked-for day with all that makes home "Sweet Home." Happy are they whose friendships all take hold upon that coming day! Happy are they who have no strong ties that are not anchored within the veil!

God has to awaken this homesickness often by breaking up our earthly net, that we may transfer our hopes to the better home. And some day we will thank Him for the flowers that He has transplanted to a climate where they will wither no more, and where God is keeping them for our arms forever.

Friend, do you know this home longing? If not, why not? Is it perhaps because your life is all invested in this earth, your interests are all committed to the present world, and it is not possible for you to have two hopes and two aims? The Christian is a man of one idea. He is living for the kingdom of the future. His hopes are all passing onward. "For where [his] treasure is, there [his] heart will be also" (Matthew 6:21).

When the gardener wants his little bedding plant to form new roots and be prepared to be transplanted to the garden, he cuts the little branch off from the stalk, and then it throws out its roots and grows into the new soil. If he did not detach it, it would never have formed its new connection or drawn its new sources of life from the soil. And so He calls upon us to separate ourselves from the hopes of earth and invest our being in the world to come. Then all the strength of our spirit will fasten around the throne and our heart will long for the consummation of its blessed hope. But there is nothing that so claims our longing for Christ's coming as Christ Himself in the heart, the Hope of glory. He is the Morning Star. As He is formed within us, so we reach out more and more for His appearing.

Friend, do you know anything of this home longing? "Blessed are the homesick," the Germans say, "for they shall get home." This is indeed true. Those that choose their portion on earth will have their reward, and those that choose it on high will in no way lose their reward. Oh, that we may be able to sing with true hearts,

> I am waiting for the coming of the Bridegroom in the air,

I am longing for the gathering of the
   ransomed over there
I am putting on the garments which the
   heavenly Bride shall wear
For the glad homecoming draweth nigh.

Oh, the glad homecoming, it is swiftly
   drawing nigh,
Oh, the sad home longing will be over
   by-and-by
Lo, the Bridegroom cometh, holy watchers
   soon will cry,
For the glad homecoming draweth nigh.

CHAPTER 7

Homecoming

*Who is this coming up from the desert leaning on
her lover? (Song of Songs 8:5)*

This is the picture of the bride's returning to
her early home on the arm of her beloved.
Soon it merges into the sweeter picture of the two
at the old home and recognizing the scenes associated with tender memories of their first meeting.
They come to the old apple tree under which they
first exchanged their vows of love. In tender, pas-
sionate devotion, she clings closer to his side and
cries, "Place me like a seal over your heart, like a
seal on your arm; for love is as strong as death, its
jealousy unyielding as the grave. It burns like
blazing fire, like a mighty flame. Many waters
cannot quench love; rivers cannot wash it away. If
one were to give all the wealth of his house for
love, it would be utterly scorned" (Song of Songs
8:6-7).

Then a little later she is represented as making
intercession for her little sister who has not yet

grown to maturity. Her little sister seems to be, indeed, unnaturally dwarfed and undeveloped, full aged, but still in form a child. But her friends answer her, "If she is a wall, we will build towers of silver on her. If she is a door, we will enclose her with panels of cedar" (8:9). That is to say, if she is a virtuous woman, closed as a wall of adamant against all the approaches of evil, we will honor and reward her. But if she is open to all comers, and loose and lax in her purity and separation as an open door, we will place around her the restraints that will perforce protect her, if need be, by the severest discipline.

This was followed by an intercession for her brothers that Solomon will give them as their inheritance his vineyard at Baal Hamon. All this is accompanied with a high-spirited protest of her own lofty virtue and devotion to her bridegroom as the grounds of his delight in her. The whole scene closes by a request from him that she will sing to him once more as in the days of old, and she responds by the sweet refrain that closes the Song of Songs. It is a refrain that carries with it enough of the notes of the old song of their early love to be recognized, but enough also that is new to raise it to a higher key and a sweeter chord. The old song was, "Turn, my lover, and be like a gazelle or like a young stag on the rugged hills" (2:17). But the new one is, "Come away, my lover, and be like a gazelle or like a young stag on the spice-laden mountains" (8:14). This beautiful closing scene of the old drama is a picture of the two stages in the Christian's journey. The first we might call going home, and the second getting home.

Going Home

The apostle expresses the meaning of this in the two words, "looking for" and "hasting unto" (2 Peter 3:12, KJV) the coming of our Lord. It is one thing to be passively drifting toward the coming of the Lord, and it is another to be going out to meet Him. This denotes an ardent expectation and an active cooperation in bringing about His advent.

1. Desiring His Coming

We may press forward to His coming first by desiring it and looking for it. It was when the people were in expectation that Jesus came of old. There is a strange power in love to draw the loved one. And when the heart of the church is really yearning for Jesus, He will speedily come.

2. Praying for His Coming

We may press forward to His coming by praying for it. This is one of the things that God has promised always to meet. Believing prayer for the Lord's return will surely not be in vain and will mightily hasten the wheels of His chariot. The Holy Spirit has Himself inspired such prayer. It is the last breath of inspiration in these sacred pages, "Amen. Come, Lord Jesus" (Revelation 22:20), even as it is the last note of the Song of Songs, "Come away, my lover" (8:14). Prayer will be made for Him continually, it is said. He comes to the heart when invited, and He will come to His own when the unanimous cry of His Bride goes up to His waiting heart.

3. Preparing the Church for His Coming

We can go out to Him by preparing for His coming, by getting ready ourselves, by putting on the wedding robe and keeping our vessels filled with the heavenly oil. Friend, are you ready? Surely if the bride were dressed for the wedding the Bridegroom would not expose her to ridicule by leaving her to wait in suspense. We believe that the moment the Church of God is prepared for the coming of the Savior He will come.

4. Preparing the World for His Coming

We can press forward His coming by preparing the world for it. This gospel of the kingdom "will be preached in the whole world as a testimony to all nations, and then the end will come" (Matthew 24:14). Those who truly long for His advent will be the most alive in sending forth the gospel in all lands.

5. Anticipating the Millennial Life

We can press forward by anticipating already in some measure the millennial life. Even here and now we may receive the foretaste of the coming kingdom. Our bodies may know a thrill of the life of the resurrection even here, and this is the meaning of divine healing. Our spirits may know a little of the rapture of His love and the marriage joy of that glad day. "We ourselves, who have the firstfruits of the Spirit, groan inwardly as we wait eagerly for our adoption as sons, the redemption of our bodies" (Romans 8:23).

Christ is coming very near today in the life of His people. There are many sober Christians who can honestly testify in these last times to a communion with the Lord which almost reaches within the veil and brings the light that is inaccessible and full of glory. Certainly the wonderful manifestation of Christ's life in the bodies of His people in the last quarter of a century is a stupendous foreshadowing of the coming glory. And the resurrection itself will only be a fuller manifestation of that which already has thrilled the mortal flesh of many of God's beloved ones. In this respect, therefore, we can go forth to meet the Lord and feel already the glad foretaste of His millennial presence.

Paralleling this back to our lovers in the Song of Songs, it is through a wilderness that she goes up to meet her lord. And surely as Christ's coming draws nearer it will become dark and lonely, and the clouds of the great tribulation will begin to gather and the violence of the latter days will give premonition of the coming crisis. But the wilderness will only press her closer to his side as she leans upon her beloved. This suggests an intimacy that well describes the deep spiritual life which is one of the characteristics of this day on the part of the few who are looking for the Lord's return. Above all others they are separated unto Him, and, having let go their hold of earthly hopes and confidences, they are compelled to lean their whole weight on Him alone.

Friend, do you know anything of this separation unto Him? Do you know anything of this expectation of Him?

Sometimes on the battlefield, when pressed by the foe, the general has been known to get upon his knees to listen for the tramp of coming reinforcements. Once it is said that, at a very great crisis in one of the decisive battles of the world, one who had thus been listening sprang to his feet and shouted, "They are coming! I hear the tramp of their feet miles away!" And the shout went along the line, "They are coming! They are coming! Reinforcements are coming!" A cheer went up, and the flag was lifted high and the lost ground recovered. The brave men held their own with enthusiasm, for they knew that the armies of help and deliverance were at hand. Are we listening for the tread of the coming feet, and do we sometimes almost hear the tramp of the armies of the sky as the procession already begins to move earthward in the advent train of the Son of Man?

Getting Home

1. Our Memories

But this picture tells us still more of the getting home. The first incident in the homecoming is the recollection of the old apple tree which had been the scene of their earlier meetings. It tells of the memories and associations that will form part of the future life and will add such exquisite sweetness to the felicities of the millennial life. It suggests to us the memories that will come back to us from the eternal shore. It suggests even more—the actual re-visiting of the scenes of earth that have been associated with our tenderest spiritual experiences.

An apple tree is not much in itself, but just such things are the pivots on which turn all that is sweetest in memory and affection in many of our lives. David speaks of his recollection of God's love in one of the Psalms in such words as these, "I will remember you from the land of the Jordan, the heights of Hermon—from Mount Mizar [or 'the little hill']" (42:6). It was this little hill which, perhaps, had no earthly name that he associated in his mind with his tenderest recollections. It was the spot where God in some way met him, delivered him, comforted him. There are spots on earth for each of us that will be eternally dear. And someday we will visit them with our precious Lord, and, remembering all the way He has led since our covenant was recorded there, we will doubtless weep for love and gratitude as we thank Him for His faithfulness. Friend, we are coming back again over this green earth and the path we are treading now. Let us leave no footprints that we would not care to retrace in company with our Lord.

2. The Perfected Love

The next deep record in the story of the home-coming is the love which it is to perfect. Then, indeed, He will set us as a seal upon His heart and upon His arm, to be separated no more forever. We will be used, even as the monarch uses his signet ring, for the highest and noblest ministries and with the very authority and majesty of the Lord Himself. And then we will love with a love as strong as death and as vehement as the love of God Himself, for when we reach His presence we will love Him even as we are loved.

3. Unselfish Consideration

Next we have a picture of service and unself-ish consideration for others. Immediately the bride begins to think of those that are dear to her, and to remember them to her lord in loving intercession. First she prays for her little sister. Who is meant by this "young sister, [whose] breasts are not yet grown" (Song of Songs 8:8), or, in other words, who with the years of a woman is still in form a child? Of course, it is a type of some class of persons who will be on earth at the time of the Lord's coming. They will be related to the real bride of the Lamb by a bond of sisterhood, but yet will be different from her in perfection and spiritual maturity. They are those who will be of doubtful purity in the judgment of the Lord. This relates to the question of whether she was a wall or a door (8:9); that is, a separated one or a loose and lax woman open to every evil influence. What is more natural than to suppose that she represents that portion of the church of Christ which will not be prepared for the Lord's coming, and which through the fault of its members willingly remains unsanctified.

It is obvious to every careful reader of the Scriptures that there will be two classes of Christians at the time of the Lord's coming. There will be the sanctified ones and the worldly and unholy followers of the Lord. The latter are His children, but His immature children who have never pressed forward to the fullness of their high calling and the true meaning of their sonship. It is of these that the apostle says, "In fact, though by this time you ought to be teachers, you need someone to teach you the elementary truths of God's word all over again. You need milk, not solid food! Anyone who lives on milk, being still an infant, is not acquainted with the teaching about righteousness. But solid food is for the mature" (Hebrews 5:12-14).

We see in the parables of the pounds and the talents two classes of servants who will come before the judgment seat of Christ. One is the faithful whose works will be rewarded as the ruler of the millennial kingdom; the other the faithless ones who have kept what they have had committed to them, but have made no use of it for Him. We see the same solemn truth also in the parable of the 10 virgins, where the foolish ones are virgins, but unprepared for the Lord's coming. We see also in the Epistle of John the distinction of two classes, one who will have confidence when He appears, and the other who will be ashamed before Him at His coming. In the book of Revelation we find the firstfruits unto God and the

Lamb who are without spot before the throne of God. Their solemn warning is to be ready for His coming and keep their garments lest they walk naked and we see their shame. We are told in Hebrews that "without holiness no one will see the Lord" (12:14).

This little sister must, therefore, represent that element which in the day of His coming will be found unready to take the place of the bride. But she is also the one for whom the bride lovingly intercedes, perhaps in the first rapture and translation of the saints, while many are still left on the earth that are dear to the translated ones. It is for this that she prays, and the Master answers that if her little sister will separate herself from the world and sin, and be a wall of virtue and purity, she will have a palace of silver. This is not surely the same as a palace of gold. It is, perhaps, an inferior reward, but certainly a glorious one. But if she is a door, that is unholy or even unseparated from the world, she will be fenced with panels of cedar, and thus will be held back by the rigid restraints of God's chastening hand from her own evil inclinations. This refers, no doubt, to the tribulations of these last days through which the remnant of God's people upon the earth will be at length separated from the world and prepared for some part indeed in the millennial kingdom.

4. *Interceding for the Others*

We find her next interceding for her brothers. These are the same brothers who had harshly treated her before. But she now asks from Solomon the least of one of his vineyards, and his royal and generous consideration. The application of this to the Jews as God's earthly people seems very clear. They, too, will have a part in the coming age. The vineyard which God's right hand had planted will be theirs again. The Queen of nations, Israel, will return to her own land and possess once more her old estates throughout the millennial years.

The general idea, however, conveyed by this picture is that of unselfishness and loving regard for the good of others. It surely implies that in the age to come God's glorified church will be engaged in high and holy ministries. We believe that our best work for God is yet to come. All we do in this day of toil and trial is to prepare for the higher occupations of that glorious time when in cooperation with Him we will rule the nations, and will see the earth under His administration, and ourselves rise to the beauty of more than paradise restored. Surely this is the meaning of such expressions as, "take charge of ten cities" (Luke 19:17); or again, "And I confer on you a kingdom, just as my Father conferred one on me, so that you may eat and drink at my table in my kingdom and sit on thrones, judging the twelve tribes of Israel" (22:29-30).

The Final Song

The last song of the bride is a note of the heavenly anthem. It reminds us that the spirit of that happy age will be the spirit of praise and that our songs will be for Him. We are going to a home where we will spend eternity in the celebration of our Redeemer's praise. The songs of heaven are but repetitions of the earth's songs with an added refrain. There are two songs in the Song of Songs: the earth song and the home song of the bride. The first song has for its refrain a minor chord, and the sad thought of the mountains of Bether, or separation ("rugged hills" [Song of Songs 2:17]). But the last song is about the mountain of Besamim, or "the spice-laden mountains" (8:14), that is love.

Oh, what a difference there will be! All the songs of earth have a touch of sorrow. It is said that the song of every bird that warbles in the air is on a minor key. All earth is tainted with the sadness of the Fall. But there is a day coming when the key will be changed and the everlasting song will be without a chorus of sorrow.

> There shall be no more crying,
>   There shall be no more pain,
> There shall be no more dying,
>   There shall be no more stain.
>
> Savior, our watch we are keeping,
>   Longing for Thee to come;
> Then shall be ended our night of weeping,
>   Then shall we reach our home.

SCRIPTURE INDEX

A.B Simpson:
A Literary Legacy

In his lifetime, A.B. Simpson wrote and published over a hundred books. Christian Publications is committed to bringing back into print all of his books that have relevance to a contemporary audience—a legacy of approximately 80 books. The titles listed on the next two pages are currently available through your local Christian bookstore.

Books by A.B. Simpson

The Best of A.B. Simpson

*The Christ in the Bible Commentary
(Volumes 1-6, Genesis to Revelation)*

Christ in the Tabernacle

The Christ Life

The Cross of Christ

Danger Lines in the Deeper Life

Days of Heaven on Earth

The Fourfold Gospel

The Gospel of Healing

The Holy Spirit: Power from on High

In Step with the Spirit

The Land of Promise

A Larger Christian Life

The Life of Prayer

The Lord for the Body

Loving as Jesus Loves

Missionary Messages

The Names of Jesus

Portraits of the Spirit-Filled Personality

Seeing the Invisible

The Self-Life and the Christ-Life

Serving the King

The Supernatural

When the Comforter Came

Wholly Sanctified

NCMC BS 1485.2 .S56 1996
Simpson, A. B.
Loving as Jesus loves